*One day your life will flash before your eyes; follow your dreams, be fearless, experiment and be curious, but most of all let go of how you think it will happen and enjoy the ride. – Natasha Davies, Because U Can*

# THE BOOK WITHOUT A TITLE
# REFLECTIONS ON LIFE AND BUSINESS

When I started my journey of entrepreneurship and self-discovery at first I hit the ground running.

I experimented by throwing myself outside of comfort and into growth, expansion. I learnt everything I had to learn about coaching and entrepreneurship. I was like a sponge soaking up all the information, learning and experience that I could, following everyone that I could learn something from. There were more than a few times it got overwhelming and difficult, but I stepped up and overcame the obstacles. There were more than a few times when I wished someone would come along and save me. I am grateful for the fact that I learnt to save myself.

I stopped following and started to lead more and to step into visibility and leadership. I reduced the amount of people I followed and started to follow only the best and the people that fitted with me. I learnt to find ways to do things with ease and to create leverage. I learnt more about myself and I learnt easier ways and the importance of following my soul and aligning with my mission. I learnt that I resisted a lot of things and started to lean into those in order to grow and expand again in different ways. I learnt to let go and to slow down, to expand into that and to sink into the presence in my own life. Striving became overwhelming and I needed to stop and slow down.

Then I found the peace that I was looking for all along. Then I found myself and I realised that this was home.

From this place I now create with ease.

What a journey, what a ride!

The journey I have travelled has been the best time of my life and totally worth all the work, now I am in such a fantastic peaceful place. I am completely aligned, completely me, completely present.

I can create magnificent things; I'm here to tell you that you can too. We overcomplicate life and business. We think way too much, yet the answers are always simple when we finally get to them.

How I created this book

I wrote this book as part of a 1000 words a day writing challenge. I wanted to create an easier way to write a book and it was: 31 days of writing, several days of editing and the book you now hold in your hands was created.

It doesn't take long to create something wonderful. It takes commitment, determination and not believing your story of can't. It takes using the pain of failure and creating the vision of the end result, then taking the steps you need to take to get there.

Even after I had written this book, I had no title. A friend read it and said 'Wow, you nearly had me in tears in places, so vulnerable'. Also, that, 'What is crystal clear is your own personal experience and not some American style you can do it ra ra offering, much deeper, thoughtful and thought provoking, from the heart.' Then another coach, whose name is also Natasha, said 'I would read your book without a title.' I am blessed to be surrounded by people like these. My heart is touched everyday by the beautiful people who are in my life. But it wasn't always this way.

You are the hero of this book. By reading it and implementing, experimenting and being curious you can create your own adventure and find your own miracles. We all perceive things differently. We look at photographs or works of art and each see something different; we describe events differently - which is why there are so many discrepancies in witness accounts. So, I will leave it up to you, the reader, to name this book. After all, it is not my place to make judgement on whether it is of use or not, it is yours. Once you have read the book I would love for you to email me your thoughts on what the title would be for you. You will find details of how to do this at the end of the book.

## Who is this book for?

What I have learnt will be useful to you if you are a coach, entrepreneur or business owner. Maybe you have just had enough of striving, have lost focus, are in self-doubt or are searching for inner peace.

In this book I cover life and business, so I am sure there is something useful here for everyone. Each chapter is a piece of writing which gives useful information and personal experience for coaches and entrepreneurs who are already in business or those thinking about starting a business.

I want to share my experience and personal discoveries with you, so that you may receive insights, learning and keep going on your journey too. Never give up, even when it gets really difficult: step up, slow down but keep going.

Build your vision and then take action every single day.

## Contents:

Chapter 1 - First my story, then my secrets

Chapter 2 - How are you holding yourself back?

Chapter 3 - The most effective way to deal with negativity

Chapter 4 - You have nothing to prove, you are good enough

Chapter 5 - Lack of time, money and energy?

Chapter 6 - Are you too available?

Chapter 7 - Someone I loved gave me a box of darkness

Chapter 8 - Clients who will sign up and clients who won't, and why you need to know the difference

Chapter 9 - Create space in your life and receive

Chapter 10 - What are you not asking for?

Chapter 11 - Sinking into your soul, presence and life

Chapter 12 - Mistakes – the pathway to ease

Chapter 13 - Financial freedom is a mindset and you can have it right now

Chapter 14 - Things can be easy when you believe that is true

Chapter 15 - Entrepreneurship can take over your life – when your passion becomes your prison

Chapter 16 - The fallacy of the inner saboteur

Chapter 17 - How to write a book, 1000 words a day

Chapter 18 - Showing up for your business and your life

Chapter 19 - One action a day – building consistency

Chapter 20 - Slow down and things show up

Copyright Natasha Davies 2016

Chapter 21 - Defining your own success

Chapter 22 - My miracle

Chapter 23 - How to create a powerful connection

Chapter 24 - What's so awful about being where you are?

Chapter 25 - Slowing down in coaching

Chapter 26 - Navigating through change

Chapter 27 - The client process

Chapter 28 - What have been the most defining moments of your life so far?

Chapter 29 - Business - too many coffees

Chapter 30 - Where to find clients

Chapter 31 - 'I'm not like these people'

Chapter 32 - Who are you marketing your services to?

Chapter 33 - Your journey takes you full circle

# **FIRST MY STORY, THEN MY SECRETS**

I left school with poor grades, as I just didn't put the effort in back then. My first jobs were in factories, shops and unskilled jobs, often finding myself jobless when factories closed. My destiny was in the hands of others.

Then I decided I didn't want it to be this way forever. I could see what sort of future was in store for me and my family, and I wanted more. I started taking evening classes, stumbled upon psychology, liked it and started learning more and more.

People I worked with and the people around me said, 'I don't know why you are bothering, it won't do you any good and will be a lot of effort wasted.' I didn't believe them; I knew it would pay off. I had discovered my longer term vision.

I volunteered as a Samaritan for a mental health charity while pregnant with my son and enjoyed that, until my father had to ring up one day and say 'Sorry Natasha can't volunteer today as she has had a baby'. I also later volunteered for another mental health organisation and travelled there every weekend to work, building my knowledge, experience and skills.

A job vacancy arose there but I wasn't successful - I didn't give up. A job vacancy became available in a local mental health charity, but I wasn't successful - I still didn't give up. Another job became available at the same charity, and I finally got the job!

## Feeling like a fraud

I had to pinch myself and didn't believe it for some time, I felt like I shouldn't be there, like I was a fraud. I know now that this was my mind keeping me stuck - I didn't listen to it. I persevered with the discomfort of this new life and found my comfort zone, expanded this, changed my life and my career prospects from unskilled jobs to professional jobs.

This step up changed my life. I continued to study, and started a degree when my son was around 4 years old. I really didn't know if I had what it would take to finish it, but took it one year at a time. I really didn't have as much belief or confidence in myself back then, but kept going and trusted that all this would pay off all the same.

I got married in 2002, then 10 months later got divorced and had to leave my family home. This was quite a difficult and stressful time, but still I continued to study. I had to deal with sorting everything out, being back under my parents' roof, a failed marriage and being a single mum again.

In 2007 I graduated with an Honours degree in Psychology as a single mum with a child, whilst working part-time for my employer - which as you can imagine was not easy. But what I have found is that nothing worth doing is ever easy, but it's definitely worth the effort.

I continued to study and to volunteer. I studied criminology, photography, law and order, Neuro-linguistic programming, psychology and volunteered for a local school and the probation service as a volunteer mentor.

I decided I would like to work with offenders and enrolled on a forensic psychology masters course at a local university. At the time I was in a difficult relationship, which I later realised was abusive, and it was hard to balance everything. Besides, I soon realised that maybe forensic psychology wasn't the path for me, as programmes were all standardised and the rehabilitation rate was only 2%. I was sure I could make more of a difference to the world and people's lives if I followed my heart with coaching.

Entrepreneurship

By this time I had set up my coaching business part-time around my job so I left the course. For a few years I worked and coached a little around my job. I was comfortable and fairly happy but my job had lost its challenge. I was comfortable but was not growing, expanding and challenging myself as much.

In December 2013 I was offered redundancy and I saw it as my opportunity to set up my coaching business full-time. I was scared, but excited. I didn't know if I would succeed, but I didn't want to spend the rest of my life wondering if I could have, either. I also got shortlisted for a job where I worked at the time - this would have been a great way to keep myself in my comfort zone, but I had already made up my mind.

## The big leap

So I took my redundancy and started my business. I started studying again at the University of South Wales on an Executive Coaching Course, as I wanted to expand my skills to maximise my success and the success of my clients. I also invested in my own coach, a Tony Robbins coach, as I had always found him to be inspiring, but also his techniques were simple to action in order to change your life. This helped me to give my business 100%.

## The pay off

I now work in that business full-time, helping people to follow their dreams, make the most of their businesses, and find happiness, significance, fulfilment and purpose, in order to enjoy their lives more. People often think that changing their lives is impossible, it is not. Anyone can start to change their lives today: it takes starting now, where you are, with what you have; it takes not listening to others, but knowing yourself and what you want or trusting that you are on the right path. You will have challenges, you will have turns, your goals will change - but the journey will be fantastic and you will be proud of who you have become.

I have become a positive, kind, happy and awesome individual, who can deal with any of life's trials and who understands how fear works, what holds you back, how you stop yourself from succeeding, what works and what doesn't.

I have created a global coaching business. I coach clients online and in person. I have also created a women's leaders network for women who inspire other women and a mastermind group for high level leaders.

I have leaned into my edge and have grown and expanded. I have shifted my mindset and now help many thousands of others to shift theirs too. I have been afraid, but I have also been fearless in spite of fear and continued anyway. I have doubted myself, but I have carried on. I identified my saboteurs and weakened them, then let them go completely to reveal the real me.

The challenges, barriers and reasons why we can't do things: these live in our heads, in the stories that we tell ourselves and the thinking that we create. We do this to keep ourselves safe, to keep ourselves comfortable and to fit in. We can kid ourselves that it's all out of our control or that circumstances control us. They do not. Two people can be in the same situation and think about things differently, feel differently and get different results.

Will you be someone who spends your life not living?

Will you give your power away by thinking you don't have any?

Will you continue to blame your circumstances, believe your story of can't and use it as an excuse to be ordinary and to have an ordinary life?

Or will you say- my time is now! I want more than ordinary, I want to reach my potential, I want an extraordinary life. Because to achieve this you have to stand out, speak up and do something different to the rest of the crowd.

To reach your potential you have to get past all of this and it's tough at times. It would be easy to give up. I am here to say don't!

Push through, keep going, trust the process, believe!

Your life will change.

I want to share with you how easy it can be, because I am on the other side and things look very different from there. I want you to get there too.

# HOW ARE YOU HOLDING YOURSELF BACK?

<u>Recognising the process</u>

<u>Fear</u>

The reason people hold themselves back is usually through fear or uncertainty. Fear of the unknown, fear of what might happen, fear of not knowing.

People jump into the past and think about what has happened before and then assume it is going to happen again. They jump into the future and create what the possibilities might be, even though they have no way of knowing because it hasn't happened yet, but then they actually create it just as they imagined. They forget to live in the present and enjoy the current moment for all that it is. After all, the current moment is all we really have. This is where life takes place.

All of this stops you from living and ensures that you just exist, not enjoying life in the fullest sense.

How are you holding yourself back from life?

## Control

Control is another aspect that comes up when people hold themselves back. They are trying to control the situation, grasping for certainty because they haven't learnt the pleasure that lies in not knowing and in being open to the possibilities. This is when the magic occurs. This is where surprise and delight exists. Why would you not want more of that?

## Story

They always have a story about why they can't do the thing that they want to do. Maybe they don't have enough time, enough energy, they are focussing on it being hard work rather than the end result or they feel they don't have the resources to make things happen.

Many people live in lack and therefore attract more lack, instead of feeling a sense of abundance.

Sometimes they feel that they don't have the opportunity or choice, but the reality is that they are holding themselves back. The thing that stands in the way of them getting what they want is the story itself, and as the storyteller then it is themselves or maybe their lack of awareness of this fact.

- So, what is your story?
- Is it really true?
- If you didn't believe that story what would be possible for you?

People often look for excuses to make themselves feel better about not achieving what they want. So that it's not their fault, but actually when we can recognise the story for what it is we can make adjustments.

There is often a lot of beating themselves up psychologically for not being able to do things, but all that self-punishment really just makes the story stick more. But, we like to prove ourselves right.

So what do you do?

1. Ask yourself.....How am I holding myself back?
2. Recognise your story and question it.
3. Is it true?
4. Are you blaming yourself or not taking responsibility for the fact that you can change things?
5. Do you believe that you can change things? Is that serving you?

6. Make adjustments. What small adjustments can you make to take you closer to your goal?

## Drop the self-punishment

We are all human beings on a journey of self-discovery and punishing yourself will just keep you stuck.

What does self-punishment or self-blame do for you? Are you worthy or good enough to receive what you want?

## What are you not receiving?

We block ourselves from receiving on lots of occasions in life. Often, again, this is to stay in control or keep ourselves safe and also in an attempt to create certainty. All of this closes down life, meaning that we experience less of it.

I'll give you an example:

Being single at the time of writing this I realised that I wasn't single through lack of opportunities, I actually had lots of those.

I even got chatted up recently by a locksmith who I had emailed about a lock I needed replacing.

I often get asked out by others - for walks, coffee, dates. I was single because I said no to all of these opportunities, because I had a story that I was waiting for the RIGHT person.

What I realised was that if I didn't explore any of the opportunities that were showing up, the RIGHT person may slip right by. I am also busy being the right person.

My focus was on what I might lose being in a relationship, rather than what that person might bring to my life. I was not receiving. I was blocking myself and holding myself back through fear and uncertainty, through running into the future and replaying the past. I noticed this and made adjustments.

- I gained clarity on what I did want
- I shifted my focus
- I became open to receive
- I explored opportunities and got curious about others

I could have carried on in my story, which I thought was keeping me safe but which was actually just keeping me stuck in my comfort zone.

I went on a date with a very nice man and had a great time, with good conversation and we had a lot in common. Opening up and exploring this felt so much better.

Do you recognise the process of holding yourself back?

What small adjustments can you make?

<u>Are you being fully present and enjoying the moment?</u>

The past is gone, we cannot change it. We have to learn to let it go, so that we can move on and enjoy the present. The future isn't created yet, but by enjoying the now and being fully present we ensure a wonderful future.

When you are present there is no fear. Fear is about what you think might happen, but hasn't happened yet. Any thoughts you might have are created and worry is like a rocking horse - it doesn't get you anywhere.

Get comfortable with not knowing. Meet people for who they are, not what you project onto them. Get to know them more deeply and in a more connected way. That way you build trust, rapport and enjoy life.

Stop trying to control everything, letting go is far more enjoyable because you live in the moment and when you do that all sorts of wonderful things occur.

Embrace fear, recognise the process and use it to your advantage. Fear isn't bad, it can also be a great motivator. Pain isn't bad, and it's where I have learnt my most powerful lessons.

Many people avoid self-reflection, fear and pain, but if you stand back and notice exactly what is happening and ask yourself a few questions then you can find your way through.

- Am I being present?
- What do I need to let go of?
- What is my story?
- What new story can I write that will serve me better?

When you do this the pressure is released instantly and you can live fully in the moment once more.

# THE MOST EFFECTIVE WAY TO DEAL WITH NEGATIVITY

Something that I struggled with for quite some time on my own journey was how to deal with negative people and comments.

I remember there was a time when I really wasn't aware that there was anything that I could do about negative influences in my life. It was only when I started achieving and learning that I really noticed it and questioned it, this was when I started to move outside of my comfort zone.

### Negativity means you are doing something right

I took up some evening classes and then people around me started saying things like 'You are wasting your time' or 'College won't get you anywhere'. I remember this made me feel annoyed - I mean it's hard enough learning new things without people putting you down. Aren't other people supposed to support you and say 'Good for you'? Luckily, many did.

I had always felt that some people around me had been glass half empty and although I got a little frustrated by this I had always been able to shake it off.

Even when I was married my husband would comment that I always had my head in books. I put this down to him being anxious that I might meet and run off with some intelligent man from university. So I guess at this point I recognised that these comments were about him, and really had nothing to do with me or my learning.

When I started on my entrepreneurial journey I started to notice it more. People asked things like, wasn't I scared taking the leap into self-employment, leaving a well-paid and comfortable job. People around me said I was 'Stupid' and 'It would never work', that there was no money out there so why would people pay me to coach them. Even though I have been in business for two years these comments still show up from others now and again.

When I've posted things on social media I've also experienced negative comments from others. When I campaigned against the sexual objectification of women these comments took on a whole new twist. I was told things like: my psychologist ex-girlfriend thinks you are crazy, to which I said, thank you; that I can't be a very good NLP Practitioner, to which I replied that I am a fantastic NLP Practitioner. They also became somewhat more threatening, with some saying that they were going to come to the protest and wave their lads magazine in my face. Most of these people experienced the BLOCK button on social media. This was how I dealt with these at the time. I did not want this kind of influence in my life.

I even blocked friends who took it upon themselves to ridicule me on my Facebook page, rather than be supportive even if they didn't believe in what I was doing. At the time it was what I needed to do and they could have supported me but agreed to disagree.

So what is the best way to deal with negativity?

We often hear that we are the average of the five main people that we surround ourselves with, and this is true. The influences in my life changed as I started to grow. I wanted to be around others who were following their dreams too. People further along than me who I could learn from.

I started unfollowing certain people on social media whose posts were negative, racist or hateful. But what about in the real world? There often isn't an unfollow or delete button that you can reach for so easily.

## Negativity has nothing to do with you

What I found was that the more I grew, the more I knew who I was and what I wanted, then the less the negative comments of others bothered me. The more I realised that these comments were their own limitations showing up, as my success was making them feel uncomfortable because if I could do it they could too, then the more I got curious about the beliefs behind these comments.

I asked:

- 'What does that do for you?'
- 'How does believing that make you feel?'
- 'What could you achieve if you believed anything was possible?'

I watched these people look inside at their own beliefs instead of looking at me. I helped them to reflect and to make their own shifts, and that served them and me a lot more. Of course, they had to be willing to do this. I also came across a lot of people who were not willing and just carried on with their negative comments. I learnt to let these people find their own way in life.

What I learnt was that whether or not people were ready to reflect on themselves was not my responsibility, it was theirs. I learnt to send these people love, bless them and release them. Not only from my responsibility, but sometimes I had to let them go from my life. Everyone is on their own journey and as I followed mine not everyone was meant to come with me. I had to let people find their own way, just as I was finding mine.

As I learnt and started to practise this, the energy in my life was less negative. I had now created space and had nothing to fill it. I realised that removing negativity meant that my social circle had contracted to virtually nothing. I knew a lot of people but hardly ever saw them. So, I started to find ways to be around positive influences. Not only on social media, but also in the real world.

## The right people

I had this idea that I needed the 'right' people. All that negativity had meant I was discounting a lot of people in my personal relationships and my work life, in an attempt to keep my environment positive and protect my energy. I had become quite isolated but I had done this to myself. Any learning is a process, so rather than reflect on the problem I got to work on creating what I wanted instead.

So, I started to open up and one day had a bit of a revelation. It's not all about me! All of a sudden I felt quite selfish. People who knew me would say I am selfless, but I had protected myself because of challenges I had with people whose story and limitations showed up.

What I realised was that as a coach to be around other people's limitations was quite exhausting, people often want help but aren't ready to invest in themselves. Many people are looking for answers, and they are looking for you to give them to them.

Sometimes even when you do they aren't ready to move yet, to let go of what they believe, as they haven't had enough learning and experienced enough pain yet to have the eureka moment. To realise that the person that needs to help them is themselves.

I learnt that I can help these people with resources, workshops and book recommendations, but I no longer work one to one with them. I only work with people who are positive, ready, willing and taking responsibility for their lives.

Other people are not your responsibility: you are your responsibility, and they are theirs.

# **YOU HAVE NOTHING TO PROVE, YOU ARE GOOD ENOUGH**

In order to write this book I created a writing challenge, where I wrote 1000 words a day for 31 days.

Initially I thought this was going to be difficult, so I said I would get up at 5am to create the extra hours needed to complete this task. The first few days I struggled with this part of my challenge: I didn't get up at 5am and I felt I had failed, even though I was still writing 1000 words a day.

I had used this method to create time to write when I had been at University. My son was small and I didn't get much time and space alone to focus on my essays, so I got up at 5am.

I remember that even back then it was hard, and that the only way I had made it work for me was to wake up at 5am just twice a week, which still created four extra hours of time and space with no distractions. I also had to be asleep by around 9.30pm, so that is what I did. This was amazing and I used this time to create all of my assignments.

This time I found it even harder to stick to the early wake up. I think I realised that writing 1000 words wasn't quite as hard a task as I had first thought, so there was no need to wake up at

5am to complete it. Also I had not done any preparation, mentally or in terms of taking my bedtime to 9.30.

## Good enough

I absolutely love achieving and reaching goals, but during my writing challenge I started to experience somewhat of a shift around this that was making me ask a few questions like:

- What am I trying to prove?
- And who am I trying to prove it too?

I started to realise that I often push myself way too hard. My high standards and drive had helped me to get where I was, but what I realised was that I need to ease up because the pushing meant that I was saying that I was not good enough yet.

I realised that actually I was more than good enough and I always had been.

This brought me back to my recent reflections and my writing.

I had recently been exploring the reasons I was single through my writing.

I was enjoying my life, I had a strong focus on my business, my family and also my own self development and I was enjoying this time.

This was my story.

The truth on reflection was that I was scared

I had this false belief that I would lose things if someone else came into my life: my freedom, my time and also that I would lose control - I mean, my life was pretty great. Everything is about good energy and positivity, what happens when someone else comes into that space?

I was looking for the 'right person' but discounting everyone as the 'wrong person'.

So, I never got anywhere. I was open to the idea but closed to the reality of it. I had been dipping into online dating apps and then dipping back out.

When I became aware of all this I realised that I had been holding myself back. So, I needed to make adjustments. I let go of all the false beliefs and the need to control the situation or keep things as they were - already things felt lighter and more open.

Then rather than judging people on the first message they sent, their profile information, pictures, occupation and education, I decided to get to know them, to get curious and reply to their messages.

I could say fear was stopping me.

Limitations were stopping me.

But, actually I knew that I would be giving up my ability to make adjustments if I believed this story and continued being in the role of a victim to my subconscious mind. Being aware and being a coach doesn't allow me to get away with these things. I hold myself accountable.

I knew that this is not true. I knew that there are no limitations, so I had no such excuse.

I got chatting to a man who lives near Newport but travels to London on business.

He talked about what he was cooking for tea: sea bass, lemon and vegetables. This was a refreshing surprise, he seemed thoughtful and open.

Just as I was on my way to bed he asked if I would like a chat.

I had realised my closedness and made adjustments around this, so I accepted and looked forward to exploring connecting with him. Before I would have declined and wanted to chat more online or maybe even not messaged him at all.

We had a fantastic conversation which covered topics such as mindset, people's attitudes, business, relationships, food, the global economy, discrimination, views about women ... the list goes on.

He seemed like a really nice person - open, honest, communicative, intelligent and interested in my interests. I was sure we could have many more amazing conversations, and if we didn't that was ok too.

Why did this conversation happen then and not before?

Because I was not open to it before.

Would we speak again? I did hope so.

Would something come of it? I didn't know, but I was learning to be more present and open in this area, which was good, and I'd get to meet some interesting people, which would enrich my life and theirs.

## What do I have to prove?

When you strive you miss a lot. Achieving is great, but there are ways to achieve with ease which also allows you to slow down and enjoy life.

Things don't have to be hard.

When I started the writing challenge I found lots of moments where I could create the space to write.

I actually wrote one of the day's 1000 words on my phone, while a plumber tested the gas appliances in a property I rent.

I wrote while I waited for clients, as I was always early for meetings so would often have 10 minutes or so to write.

We can often make use of these moments to tick off tasks from our lists, freeing up time to enjoy life a little more. We don't need more time; we just need to make use of the small moments more effectively.

These are moments we lose when we strive, when we are chasing something and we miss what was there all of the time. We always have time right under our noses, we just need to notice it.

I have proved I can achieve many things; I have worked on myself and know that I am good enough. I know that there is no failure only feedback and I have found ways to find ease and leverage.

I have overcome challenges and created wonderful things. I have created a global coaching business and supported many clients, but I must remember that it's not all about achieving for them too and so go even deeper with them to reach new levels of understanding and possibility.

Moving to a different level is not always about moving forward or moving up, slowing down and going deep is also important. Everyone is already good enough; no one has anything to prove to anyone.

The moment we start trying to prove things to ourselves and others we lose things. We lose our connection with ourselves, we close ourselves down and we lose the connection with others and all the things that make living in the present moment a joy.

- What are you trying to prove?
- Who are you trying to prove it to?

## I have all that I need

I now understand that I have all that I need and have nothing to prove, but I do like to expand and grow from a position of good enough already. Right now I want to open up and connect more in some areas of my life: mainly the ones where I notice I am more closed and I can't push myself hard all the time and do that.

I also need to slow down and connect more in business, too. Even though I have been connecting with lots of people the focus has been on striving and achieving, working collaboratively to make things happen rather than really getting to know people on a deeper level.

This needs adjustment, too. It's great to make things happen, but connecting more deeply is important, too. Balance is important.

Maybe striving kept me in my comfort zone, maybe I thought I was in control, but keeping things the same is not growth and actually nothing stays exactly the same, so being fluid and open to change is important. Change is always happening, progress is another thing.

This is what I'm realising and also that slowing down, letting go and coming from a place of good enough I still get things done.

I still achieve more than most people and now I do it from a much better place too.

- How can you open up to life more?
- How do you push yourself too hard?
- You have nothing to prove you are good enough

# **LACK OF TIME, MONEY, AND ENERGY?**

No time, money, energy story

We all have the same amount of time, but many of us use the story that we don't have enough. We are in lack not only when it comes to time but also other resources too: energy, money, knowledge, I could go on.

It's a common story. I would really love to do X, Y and Z but I really don't have the time.

Do you recognise it?

However, the reality is that everyone has the same amount of time but we all use it differently. There is an abundance of all of these things all around us, but while we are in our story of lack we don't notice how much abundance we have.

Not enough

We are focussed on 'Not enough' rather than 'Unlimited'.

And yes, our time on earth is limited in a sense but your perception of it will affect how you use it. So, for some people who are 50 they feel that 60 is such a long way away. For others it's closer than they would like. This is down to perception.

When you are always in a rush time slips away and you never get to do the things that are important, maybe you spend time doing other things that aren't important.

It really comes down to how we use the time, money and energy that we have. When I worked in my employment I would come across some people who said they had no money, but actually they had more money than the staff that worked there who did a lot more with what they had, so again it's down to perception and what you do with what you have.

I know people who don't work because of ill health but who enjoy holidays and whose houses are always immaculate. I know others who work very hard and have a lot of financial resources but don't have time for holidays and haven't bought new furniture in years.

Priorities

It's all about priorities. I know people who don't have much in the way of financial resources, but what they do have they spend on developing themselves and their learning, and that is their focus; I know others who never spend any time or money in this area.

I come across many people who live in lack of all of these things, but to someone else's standards they are in abundance. Just as some people who are laid-back in personality seem to have all the time in the world, while others are in a state of stress and panic that they don't have enough.

This all begins with you!

There are people out there who have less time, money and energy than you, who are happier than you are and who are experiencing life more fully.

This is something that we don't often realise: it is never the situation but how we perceive it. How do you perceive time, money and energy? How can you change the way you view these things?

When it comes to energy, certain activities drain your energy

Do you sit in front of the television a lot? Do you eat big heavy meals? I attended an event last year where we were in a room for 14 hour days, but we periodically got up and jumped around - this taught me that you can create energy, even when you feel quite exhausted. Music is another way to create energy and lift your mood.

Copyright Natasha Davies 2016

- How can you create energy?

- Or do you believe the story that you just don't have enough?

That it's beyond your control.

The story you tell yourself affects your energy too.

How much is enough?

Time, money and energy: where is your standard?

To some people a few hours, £50 and the energy to get through the day is enough; to others it's a few months, a million pounds and the energy to run a marathon. What is your standard?

How much time, money, and energy would you be happy with?

You may find it's less than you think. Most people want to be comfortable financially, have enough time to do the things they want to do and have the energy to do them.

Do you spend these resources on things that are important to you or that will give you the best return on your investment?

A lot of people spend their resources on things that aren't going to take them any closer to their goals, they spend them doing things for others and forget about their own needs. Serving others and not yourself means you aren't practicing self-care.

In terms of money its well-known that poor people buy stuff, middle class people buy liabilities and wealthy people buy investments.

Younger people are spending their money on experiences and looking for events to spend their time in more and more.

What is really important to you?

- What are your priorities?

- Will they take you closer to your goals?

Writing this book was one of mine. I wanted to create content to reach and serve more people; I also discovered how much I enjoy writing. How I had forgotten that I wrote poetry from childhood and facilitated writers groups through my work.

We have all heard of the Pareto principle or the 80/20 rule: if you haven't it states that 20% of your effort results in 80% of your rewards.

You can use this principle in all these areas of your life. Spend your money where you will get the greatest rewards, spend your time and energy doing the things that bring you the greatest enjoyment.

In business spend your time doing things that put you in front of your potential customers. How much business do you get and how many customers do you reach in each of the business activities that you take part in? Some will be more fruitful than others.

So, where you spend the resources is important and really can make a huge difference to the quality of your life. It can make a huge difference to your business, too.

You can discover the answers through some exploration.

Write down all of the activities that you take part in and rate them in terms of the rewards/results that they create.

So, for example, if you like to take walks in the countryside and on a scale of 1-10 this gives you an 8 in enjoyment, then do more of that.

If you run a business and all of your clients have come from networking, but you spend most of your time on social media where only one of your clients came from, then spend less time on social media and more time networking. It really is that simple, but we often don't notice when we are leading busy lives.

You need to slow down, then you can discover:

The 20% of customers who bring the greatest income to your business.

The 20% of time that creates more growth in your business.

The 20% of time that is more productive.

The 20% of activity that creates the most energy.

This could be expanded into other areas and it means you can then focus more of your time and effort in these areas to create leverage, ease, joy and happiness in your life.

So, where is your 20% and why aren't you focussing your efforts there?

Some people spend all their time doing activities that bring very little happiness. If this is you maybe some adjustments are needed?

Even if you adjusted one thing every week, you would soon have a much happier life or more productive business.

## So, start right there with one thing

The great news is that once you notice these things you CAN make those adjustments and start being more productive in life and business, which can only bring a positive result.

Most people know about this principle, yet we often need reminding to refocus our efforts where it matters the most.

## **ARE YOU TOO AVAILABLE?**

Today I had a revelation, about my being so visible on social media, as I'm always online. I post probably 30-50 posts a day across all of my networks. I get hundreds of notifications and lots of messages daily, I am therefore always available.

Today while I was having around three conversations, while trying to clean up and sort out my 3 year old, I understandably got overwhelmed.

This got me thinking.

Who decided I needed to be available 24 hours a day for my followers, prospective clients and clients?

I mean, is that realistic? My clients don't expect it. I suppose I did, maybe, to provide value, but I have always provided value through my coaching.

What I also realised is that most of the posts I make aren't yielding results in terms of people approaching me for coaching. This usually happens through blogging or public speaking.

So, why am I spending so much time doing it? Also, this is not how I imagined my life to be when I became a coach.

## Giving too much

Like most coaches I am giving too much in the wrong places. I mostly post on my private and business pages, and in a few groups other people run, but I also have my own groups and actually post there less. Then it hit me: shouldn't I be concentrating on the individuals who have already showed a willingness or interest in my groups by joining them, instead of posting more to the majority of people who haven't moved from just being in my friend's or in other people's groups?

When people contact me I used to answer everyone, now I just answer enquiries and people I have had some contact with, although I still get people who aren't ready to invest in coaching but want to chat.

As coaches we sometimes give time to these people so as to be in service, yet many of them aren't yet ready or willing to move themselves.

Coaches are often givers, but if we give to the people who aren't ready then we have no time to give to the people who are ready and who are the people who invest in themselves and, ultimately, pay us for and value our services.

There will always be people who want to pick our brains or chat for free.

Copyright Natasha Davies 2016

The people who we post on social media for but who aren't ready get to falsely feel better when they see our quotes, meaning they have no need to approach us. We make them feel good. Just enough so that they feel short-term relief.

Help them to create their vision

What I have discovered with coaching is that people who invest have to be able to see what it would provide.

Such as:

A vehicle to get them from where they are now to where they want to be.

Many of these people don't yet know where they want to be, mainly because they are focussing on the pain and they haven't yet built the pleasure or the vision or they don't yet believe in the possibilities.

So, when I meet potential clients I always check where their focus is and whether they have a vision or a dream for what they want to create.

Now sometimes they don't and that's ok because they are willing to explore it or because they have had enough of pain and are willing to trust the process and try something new.

But if they aren't willing to do any of this or are looking for answers then, in my experience, they aren't ready to be coached.

Coaching requires responsibility and action so I only coach those who are ready for this and often turn people away who aren't.

Back to reflections on visibility

Online everyone is saying 'be more visible' but if everyone is doing the same thing maybe we should not just blindly follow the crowd but do something different.

This is how I think, question everything!

I've reflected on this for a while and I'm feeling like this damages the coaching business.

Free coaching

I mean, if I need a coaching session I have hundreds of coaches all lining up to serve my need for free. I can easily have one coaching session a week if I want, albeit from different coaches. My social media feed is full of coaches posting feel good quotes so I may never need those coaching sessions after all.

Many people are happy as long as they are comfortable.

Of course, many also have more ambition to create the life they want and these people are my clients.

So, if people who are happy with comfort or not happy with discomfort, but who are not unhappy enough to do anything about it are not the target audience I am aiming to attract ... then why am I posting so much to the majority of people?

So here is what I have decided to do:

1. Stop posting endless quotes, be more targeted in what I post towards my ideal clients
2. Spend the time writing blogs targeted towards my ideal client
3. Post more in my own groups and not as much on my private page
4. Post my blogs on LinkedIn
5. Share my website more
6. Share more about the value of coaching and how it can help and be of service to my ideal client

When you are so readily available why would anyone invest in coaching? They are often under the illusion that chatting and coaching are the same. They are not. People really step up and start moving when they invest in themselves.

So, in order to serve people better, I'm making a distinction between coaching and chatting. Everyone enquiring about coaching gets a questionnaire, if they don't complete it and send it back I don't see them. If people want a chat, it's a chat and no coaching.

Providing value

Why do coaches feel that they have to provide so much upfront value, maybe because they don't value themselves? I have learnt to value myself and my service, but I was in a pattern and didn't even notice. It was only when it got overwhelming that I took the action and one day I just turned off my phones.

First I felt a relief like a weight had been lifted. I was being available for everyone, even people I didn't know, but not being available for me.

Then I noticed the calmness, how I felt lighter, how my home felt calmer. I mean, I've had thousands of people in my space for a long time.

Then I noticed how it was such a beautiful day outside. Life wasn't happening inside my phone or on social media, it was happening all around me. Only, I wasn't participating because I was being always available for total strangers, just in case they were a potential client.

I will always be available for my clients and they usually email me or message me if they need to change appointments or if they need to speak with me, but they do not want to chat. They get my undivided attention in our sessions.

This is how it should be. Coaching is my work, not my life. Life is happening outside of coaching and outside of social media.

This was a big insight that changed everything for me.

Reflections

I think it is better if I am only available in my groups, through my business page, via my website or in person for potential clients.

Maybe I need to separate business from personal on social media, as mine have been combined.

This would be clearer for potential clients, as well as for me.

As for huge visibility, I'm leaving it behind and being a lot more focused in what I post. I'm also sometimes going offline on messenger so I can focus on my life and separate the business aspect, otherwise it's all day and all night. I answer clients straight away and serious enquiries, but often leave my phone for long periods while I enjoy life.

After all, that is what I help others to do too.

What this is making me realise is that when something is always available it's less desirable. So, if you want to be more desirable then be less available.

A wise coach once told me if you want to be sought after disappear off social media and people will come and find you.

Someone once searched for me for a year when I left my job. They became a client.

Ask yourself are you too visible/available for your own good?

# SOMEONE I LOVED GAVE ME A BOX OF DARKNESS

<u>I saw the gifts</u>

When I was in an abusive relationship I didn't know I was in an abusive relationship. I wasn't aware or awake to the fact.

I have to say it crossed my mind once or twice but I always dismissed it. I wasn't ready to admit that it was just that. Maybe because I would have to take some action, maybe because I might blame myself or maybe because it was hard to let go of something that had been a part of my life for so long.

Maybe I would have to admit I was wrong and others were right?

Either way, the pain of changing it seemed greater than the pain of staying in it, or in a way it was. When it ended then I was faced with loss.

It wasn't all bad; there were some really great things too. I laughed such a lot at that time and I really felt loved. I also cried a lot and felt unloved.

Copyright Natasha Davies 2016

## A double edged sword

It was like a double edged sword, that when it was good it was really good and when it was bad it was really bad. It was very confusing and an emotional roller coaster at the time.

These days I don't really think about it, I've moved on so much and I've let go of anything that I was still holding onto, because for a long time I did just that and at times it was a difficult journey.

I was letting go of the bad bits but I was still holding onto the good bits. Maybe even being in judgement of these being either good or bad didn't help, but when you realise that it's designed that way and that none of that was ever about you, but it was all about the other person, it makes it easier to let it go.

## Forgiveness

Forgiveness of the other person and forgiveness for yourself is important in letting go, too.

I talked about it, I reflected on it. I was still attached to it as being part of my journey, my past. I was focussed on moving away from it and avoiding that sort of thing ever again.

Then I focussed on myself and I started to grow, I began to know myself, know what I wanted in life, to love myself for who I was and who I could be.

I began creating my future, helping others and following my dreams. I realised that in my relationships, whether romantic or otherwise, that a lot of other people's stuff shows up.

It's all about them

A person's abuse, negativity or comments is so much about them and not about the other person at all. I was able to let go.

There was nothing I could have done differently and another person's actions and thoughts were not my responsibility.

I was starting to surround myself with the people who were positive and supportive, and letting go of the ones that couldn't be happy for me, mainly because they weren't happy with themselves.

That's right, I was taking responsibility for things that weren't mine to take. So I stopped all of that and focussed on my own path and what I could offer.

## Focussing on your own journey is important

When I did this the past faded away and I no longer focussed there. I gave myself permission to let go. I now have no attachment to it and I see the gifts in the experiences I had and how it has made me who I am today. How I have made me who I am today.

## Be present

More recently I have been shifting my focus to the present, enjoying life today, every moment of it and it's magical. Having fun, being playful and curious about the world. Feeding my soul, being present and in alignment with myself and my goals.

This is where the juice of life is. This is where you touch your soul and you feel both longing and belonging in an intricate dance. This is where love resides.

## Love

Love for yourself and love for others, even those you have to bless and release because they are at a different stage in their journey and are not meant to travel with you on yours.

The past is full of lessons but you can't change it, you can only perceive it differently. The future is full of exciting possibilities but it's what you do today and every day that creates that future - the actions that you take consistently, day in day out.

It's who you are being and the actions that you take on a minute to minute basis that defines what enters your life.

You can change a whole day with a smile that shines out to the world like a beacon. You can change a whole week with an idea in creation. You can change your body chemistry with a walk or a power stance.

Yes, I was in an abusive relationship, I know that now, but I didn't want to stay there which is why I stopped talking about it and shifted my focus to what I wanted to create instead, because talking about it changes your day, week and body chemistry too.

Why am I talking about it now?

I'm talking about the process of it. I'm detached from it because I let go of holding onto it and I still think it's a useful share to help others, but I'm no longer a victim to it.

I can talk about it just as I would talk about the process of cooking a meal or the process of writing an essay.

It holds no emotion for me anymore, because I worked through it and let it go. Because I shifted my focus not by learning to avoid those sorts of people (which is what I tried to do at the start) because holding your focus there only means you see more of those.

We get what we focus on. So I focussed on me, my dreams, my growth, my happiness and my life. I focussed on my business, my family and my clients.

In this space I am meeting some really wonderful people. Being open and not attached to any outcomes I have slowed down.

I used to be in such a rush with relationships and I couldn't be alone. Now I love my own company, solitude and time to do the things I like to do.

I am never alone even when I am alone. It's an amazing place to be. I am fulfilled; I am achieving my full potential and stretching myself. I am happy, loved, most of all I accept myself for who I am and know that I am good enough.

Maybe all of this would not have happened if I had not been given that box of darkness or if I had not seen the gifts.

If you are ever given a box of darkness....

Turn it around........Because u can.

# CLIENTS WHO WILL SIGN UP AND CLIENTS WHO WON'T, AND WHY YOU NEED TO KNOW THE DIFFERENCE

Your clients are all around you

We can all get a little stuck in our thoughts about how to find our ideal clients and often start this mission with the HOW question.

How can I get or find clients? It is never about what you can get and it is always about what you can give.

Or the WHERE question.

Where can I find the clients who will benefit from and invest in my services? The answer to this is everywhere. You never know who you are sitting next to until you have a conversation.

Asking these questions is how we close down the possibilities. Being open to delving a little deeper with the people that you meet is part of the answer.

Sometimes we can be in a room full of people and say these are not my clients, but be curious - get to know people and serve them and you may find that some of them are.

Bear in mind: are they ready, are they willing to explore and do they have a vision or are willing to explore one? Also, always ask permission to coach.

Each time you say, 'they are not my client', you discount people who could be.

On the other hand, a person has to have a certain type of mindset to invest in the higher fee services.

Some people are in short term mindset, looking for information and taking advantage of free mode.

Maybe because they feel they can't afford the resources or time to invest more fully, maybe because they think if they get the information they can do it on their own.

What they don't realise is they can, but it takes longer and it's more of a struggle to do it that way.

I know because I have been there

Others have already realised the benefits of investing in themselves and in working with a coach who understands the processes and has been through the bumps themselves, so the client doesn't have to, and who can help them to find their own way more quickly and safely than they maybe could alone.

To help them stay motivated when they hit the tough times and to create the space to explore the possibilities so that they can move forwards with enthusiasm and ease.

Someone who knows that you don't have to go miles to find someone who you can be of service to; you don't have to find people who have lots of resources, just people who make themselves and their success and development a priority. People who have a dream and are already pursuing it. People who you can help to get out of their own way.

People who have hit a challenge and need reminding that if they get out of their thoughts and do what they love that the path is actually clear.

People who invest in coaching do, however, have some similar attributes:

1. They are in growth or they have had enough of struggle
2. They are willing or eager
3. They have an abundance mindset or are willing to work on developing one
4. For them, money may have become less important while reaching their potential, as being happy has become more important
5. They often know there is more out there for them

6. They know the answers lie with them, they take responsibility

People who don't often invest in coaching:

1. See it as a cost
2. Have a lack mindset
3. Are fixed and like comfort
4. Money is important but mostly spent on feeling better in the short term
5. Short term mindset and instant gratification
6. They are looking for answers outside of themselves, so they don't think they have any control

Of course there are all sorts of people in between, too. As with any dichotomy there is a middle ground, but this idea may be useful to you.

Everything starts from you

The other thing is that everything starts from you. So if you are closed, eliminating people based on criteria, this doesn't help. I mean, if you are a coach who works with women over 40 then obviously that's your bracket and you would look within that group.

But being open to anyone who is a woman and over 40 would be good, so not judging if the person is or isn't a possible client until you have explored this a little deeper.

Be in service to them and see if it feels right, if you are a good match. They can also see if you are a good match of coach for them.

As you coach people you will feel when the time is right to propose a coaching relationship.

Quick fix

Sometimes people come to coaching because they want a quick fix to a problem and a few coaching sessions can get them to a place where they don't need a coach.

They are being pushed by the pain of the problem and so are in a short term mindset. In my experience these people are not ready to commit to long term coaching to create a future goal, because they aren't focussed on that but on removing or moving away from the pain.

Help them to build the pleasure of what they really want and to know why they really want it by exploring their deeper why and they are then seeing the possibilities and have a vision for what coaching could help them to create.

Which clients would excite you

It is a good idea to know who would be the clients that really excite you to work with them, so that you can not only attract them but notice them when they arrive.

After delving into who would really excite me to work with them I posted two social media posts for women leaders who inspire other women and received 170 responses from people who identified with the profile that I put out.

This required creating space and doing that inner work first to create that outer magic so clarity is a great force. Also intention, as I only had the intention of connecting and nothing else, but from that came other things: collaboration, groups and mutual support.

Women helping women, coaches helping coaches: helping each other up.

Not everyone is meant to be your client - some will become mentors, some friends, some collaborators, some you will meet and let go, but the more connections that you make, the more of all of these different people you will meet and some will become your clients too.

You can get what you want by helping others to get what they want.

## **CREATE SPACE IN YOUR LIFE AND RECEIVE**

Creating space is about creating time for you, but there are also lots of other areas of your life where you can create space too.

Your home:

De-clutter, give things away, create some extra income, move furniture around, thin out your belongings and create space.

You'll be surprised how wonderful that feels. Stop buying things that you don't really need. Learn to live with less stuff. Even clearing out cupboards creates space to store things in a more organised fashion or maybe that newly uncluttered under-stairs cupboard can be used for another purpose - a reading nook, which you always wanted, or that second bathroom.

Your car:

Empty your door pockets, remove that spare pair of shoes, clear out the boot and the glove box.

Our cars sometimes collect clutter and litter, particularly the door pockets and boot. Sort out your CDs. Give it a spritz of polish and it's as good as new. We spend a lot of time in our cars travelling to and fro, so make sure it's an enjoyable space.

Your garden:

The garden is a wonderful place to kick back and relax, so create some space.

Clear out weedy plant pots. Clear up the leaves. Pick up those toys and send them back to the shed. Power-wash that patio, add some twinkly lights and you have an evening haven, too.

Add some inspiring props, make a pergola or build your own outside space where you can enjoy being outside in all weathers.

Your mind:

Let go of those beliefs that aren't serving you. Dump the negative thinking and self-doubt.

Be present and start to enjoy the moments in every day.

Create a positive affirmation that celebrates your strengths, your journey and creates direction for future growth. Look past excuses and the limitations you create, think positively, and spur yourself on. Change the way you think and things will change.

The people you hang out with:

The people you spend time with can have a big impact on you and your energy. Other people's problems are not your responsibility. Obviously be there for your friends, but if you have some that take more than they give, sap your energy or don't give anything back, let them go. Find people who lift you up: the givers and matchers in life. Not everyone is meant to complete your journey with you. Create space for some really great people.

Your office:

De-clutter your office, make it an inviting place to be, an inviting place for your customers to be. A few quality motivational quotes can give some interesting reading.

Remove unnecessary leaflets and magazines. Clear out storage cupboards and get rid of unwanted paperwork. Create streamlined systems and processes to create more ease while working. Take your work outside now and then. Work in the park, say against a tree, to create an outside office.

Your quiet writing/reading/creative space:

Create a space to feed your soul. Somewhere elevating with no distractions where you can be alone, reflect, journal, read and be in solitude with yourself. Somewhere you can get some space from the distractions of life. An internet free zone, where you can be present, meditate, practice yoga or simply be.

In nature:

Enjoy the space of the countryside. Be in nature. Go for walks, spend time by the water whether a river or the sea. Feel the wind in your hair, gaze at the night sky, and feel connected to something bigger than yourself. Create space for yourself out in the open air, not for work but for personal time.

Your fridge:

Create space in your fridge for healthy snacks, vegetables and fruit. Create space in your freezer for home-made meals and frozen-yoghurt lollies.

Create space in your cupboards and replace unhealthy snacks with more nutritious alternatives. Give the fridge and cupboards a spring clean; get rid of old Tupperware, odd plates and cups. Keep the minimum that you need.

Your inbox:

Unsubscribe from unwanted emails. Delete old messages. Organise your computer into easy to find folders. Turn up your junk mail filters and clean your PC. Clean your disc and free up some space. Have a splurge on annoying messages that are taking up time in your day.

Your phone:

We all have lots of media, notes and texts that can be cleaned up and slimmed down. Delete old messages and texts, remove unwanted apps. Upload images to a cloud based storage and delete them off your phone, to free up space and no longer see the storage full message.

Your wardrobe:

Have a charity clothes swap with friends or run a clothing tabletop sale. List clothing items on an auction site or give them to your local charity shop. Clear out anything that you haven't worn, that doesn't fit or any broken items. Sort out all of those odd socks. Thin out your accessories, hats, scarves, belts, bags. Give bags to your local homeless shelter with spare toiletries in.

Your shoes:

How many pairs of shoes do you actually wear? Clear out any that you haven't worn for some time. Organise them so they are easily accessible, colour code them, store them properly in an organised manner. Give some away or sell them, then buy just one new pair with the proceeds.

Toys:

Clear out all of your unwanted toys. Maybe your child has grown out of them, or collected lots of little toys from food outlets or magazines. Sort them into boxes and, again, store them in order.

Electricals:

Have two hair dryers, straighteners, MP3 players or hoarding old phones? Recycle them; list them on Freecycle or eBay. Throw out any broken ones.

Create time:

Create time in your day to do what matters most. What makes you happy? Feel good about creating this time for you, whatever that is. Have a coffee in a local cafe. Attend an event, walk, read, and learn. Just sit and do nothing. Slow down, relax and recuperate. Fill yourself up and do it consistently. Schedule it and make it part of your daily routine.

Creating space anywhere in your life leaves room and creates an opening for new things to enter, even if that new thing is just space. Often when you do this, magic occurs.

# WHAT ARE YOU NOT ASKING FOR?

In life and in business

As a coach I am always in service to others, so after a meeting recently where I gave to and served a connection I walked away wondering what I'm not asking for?

I'm a giver so whenever I meet people I want to serve them. People often walk away with contacts, useful information and generally easier ways to do things. I want to leave people feeling lighter than when they arrived.

To me getting things done is simple, because I know how to create a clear path, so for others to have a clear and easy path is a gift.

After this particular meeting, while I was walking away, it hit me that as a giver there are lots of things that I'm not asking for.

- Referrals

- Contacts

- People to share things on social media

- Help

- Information

- <u>Receive too</u>

We givers also need to be able to receive, that is how the universe flows. However, there is so much we won't be receiving if we never have the courage to ask for what we want.

There were so many things I wasn't asking for. So, I reflected on the difference that asking could make.

I've had some magical moments asking for things.

While on a coaching intensive I asked a lady if she would like me to take her photograph, she was suspicious, then delighted and curious.

I asked a family if I could borrow one of their bicycles and they said 'yes that one is your size'.

I asked a man if I could have a picture with a helicopter that he was looking after, he said yes, took my picture and then had a deeply connected and vulnerable conversation with me. He said 'someone sent you today didn't they?'

## Asking for coffee

I asked if my Facebook friends would like to buy me a cup of coffee and received around 25 responses. I drank a lot of coffees that month.

Asking creates magic. It creates an icebreaker for a deep conversation. When we ask for what we want, we give others permission to ask for what they want also.

So, my insight was that I really need to do so much more asking.

I asked for a free book at a networking event and I got a yes.

## What else can I ask for?

I asked for money off a bed for my son and free delivery, and I got that too.

What are you currently not asking for that would make a big difference in your life or business?

I've decided that I am going to ask for people to share more of my posts on social media, to share and like my page, and to follow me on other networks.

I am going to ask people if they know anyone that I could be of service to right now.

Copyright Natasha Davies 2016

I am going to ask for a fee for my consultations. I'll offer a free 10 minute session to establish a client's needs and how I can help, and then offer them a consultation or coaching session with a minimal fee.

In business customer acquisition is a big cost, yet most coaches offer free coaching sessions up front - particularly high ticket coaches.

I realised that I had felt that I needed to prove my worth to potential clients, but that actually clients who have a free session get a lot of value out of this.

I was not valuing what I provided; I was not valuing myself and my time, so how can I expect potential clients to.

I decided to step up and change the copy on my website to reflect this. Sometimes as a giver we can give too much.

Often offering free consultations has helped people to see the value and helped me to see if potential clients are a good fit, but it doesn't make a lot of business sense when you get a few people who aren't ready to commit to coaching or aren't a good fit.

There are travel costs, office costs, time and energy spent. As a coach I would justify this by saying 'but I feel good having helped them' or ' they just aren't ready' or 'maybe I could have served them more fully'.

I needed to step up and realise that, just as one of my clients said, 'I hope you see the value in what you provide, you change lives' and that has got to be worth more than free.

## The value of free

Often people don't value a free service as much as they do when they invest resources. So, by charging a fee I am also encouraging them to invest in themselves, and I know that is the route to a better life, a change of mindset and all sorts of magical experiences.

There is a very important mindset shift from lack to abundance and gratitude, from cost to investment. Poor people buy stuff, middle class people buy liabilities and wealthy people invest. It means you get more value for your money.

## We are surrounded by consumerism and stuff

Often people who say they don't have enough money can save a substantial amount if they stop buying stuff.

Liabilities like cars and houses actually cost you money.

Investments mean your money grows. When people invest in themselves they increase their opportunities to create more time, energy, money, possibilities and to enjoy life and grow their businesses. So, investment property, investments, coaching and creating products. There is no amount of stuff that will do that.

Are you asking for stuff? Do you want more stuff?

Are you wanting or needing liabilities, things that will help you to keep up with the Joneses but things that will cost you money?

Or, are you investing your money so that it grows, investing in yourself so that you grow? Are you asking for more for yourself?

When you ask you can shift up a level in your asking, too. Stretch to bigger requests, chase the no's. Lean in and reach out further than you have been. Grow in your asking. Ask for things that feel uncomfortable.

Every time I ask for something and get a yes that surprises me, the question I ask myself is 'what else can I ask for?'

# **SINKING INTO YOUR SOUL, PRESENCE AND LIFE**

When I was a child and in my early teens I was a soulful thinker, always dreaming and contemplating around life. I loved space and often would be sitting in my room reading. I spent most of my days outside.

I would walk home from school in the rain as a teenager and, when I got to the lane that took me to my house, I would take off my shoes and step in each puddle along the way, feeling the cool water between my toes. Feeling the rain on my face and being present in the moment.

Sinking into my soul was probably my favourite pastime. Slowing down and experiencing life more fully was my default mode.

When I hit my later teens things got faster paced. There was always somewhere to go and things to do. Everything became more of a rush.

When I started work my days were filled with people, work and speed, as my first few positions were on production lines in manufacturing. There were targets, clocking-in machines, conversations, and you worked to live. Life happened by the clock. Every week we wished for Friday, every month we wished for payday.

After that my positions were in customer service and community organisations, so again I was always around people.

I was always busy doing and completing tasks and having conversations. My work in mental health taught me to be more present, as I worked a lot with one to one with clients. When I got home there were tasks to complete like housework, cooking and putting my son to bed.

Things to do in self-employment

When I became self-employed, again, there was so much to do. As an entrepreneur you wear many hats and with two children at home that kept me busy, too. As I moved along the entrepreneur's journey I began to realise that I needed time for myself to feed my soul.

I was the centre of my business and without me it wouldn't work. So self-care and time for me became more important.

It's easy in life to get caught up in the doing, the tasks, the housework, family, business, work and the to-do list. People often reach a point where they wonder if this is all there is.

## Stop glorifying busy

The problem is that we are all going so fast that we are not at all present in these activities. We have so much going on that we move quickly from one activity to the next without realising that we are rushing our lives away.

Time is our most important commodity and yet we speed through it like it's a race to the finish.

We always wish we were further along than we actually are or that it's summer, Saturday or the evening so we can relax.

We can always get more money, but we can never get more time. Each moment is a precious gift, but we often don't give it the importance it deserves. Time is your life ebbing away, use it wisely. Enjoy it, every second.

If you want to do something do it, if you have a dream follow it, but always be present in whatever you do. Savour it, immerse yourself in it. Follow your passion and feed your soul.

When we rush we are bypassing our connection with others and our connection with ourselves - the connection with our own soul.

As a teenager I was connected to my soul so much more.

What was different then? I had space. I slowed down. I took part in soulful creative activities: reading, writing, contemplating, sitting in silence, solitude.

The further I got on my journey the more I realised that these activities were not just as important, but actually more important than the task based activities.

You see we are on this earth for a short amount of time and it's too short not to live each moment being present.

Gradually I became more and more present in more and more moments. I could always shift into presence or into action when needed, but realised that presence was where I needed to be all of the time and everything else works from there.

When you slow down and sink into your soul you notice more, feel more, and enjoy more. All of that rushing means you miss all of that. So what are you missing out on?

When you slow down the things you were striving to get done, because you had an idea of the one way that was going to happen, don't get forgotten, they happen anyway but in different ways because now you are open to more possibilities.

It sounds totally illogical and you still have to take action, but it's much slower and sometimes things just appear, maybe because you have created space. You have let go. You are being a different energy and so attract different things towards you.

When you slow down you become happier. When you can let go of having to control everything life becomes lighter. There is less to think about. You start to have more fun. You let go of any thoughts that caused you worry, anxiety and anger.

When you slow down, sink into your soul and are present, when you make that the most important thing and let go of everything else you are at peace with yourself.

Striving and not good enough

Striving and trying to get somewhere because you aren't there yet are often indicators that you don't feel you are good enough or are trying to prove your worth. Yet the only thing you need to be is present and to slow down. Be present in everything you do. Take your time doing it. Enjoy it. Really experience everything in life.

Do less to receive more. Sink into your soul and be happy. Happiness is always there, but often we are reaching for another place so much that we don't notice it was always available, if we just slowed down to meet it. To meet ourselves.

This place is where our best work is done. This place is where we find ourselves. This place is where real life happens. Life isn't happening in our heads, on our social media, in our Smart phones.

It's happening in every moment that we breathe, it happens in our gratitude for those moments. It happens looking into our children's eyes, walking on a mountain, sitting soulfully alone in solitude or the moments that you spend with others connected by each other's presence.

So stop with the huge to-do lists, as that's the way to burnout or an early grave. Stop wishing you were somewhere else and enjoy where you are right now.

Do a few things really well and always be where you are with presence. Live each moment. Be connected to yourself and others. Create space to sink into your soul.

Create space to show up in totally and as you. Create silence for accidental discovery. Some of my best ideas come to me while in this space.

Because there is so much more of life happening when you sink into your soul.

# MISTAKES – THE PATHWAY TO EASE

Mistakes can often open up opportunities, but you will never know if you are afraid to make them or if you follow all the rules.

People often fear making mistakes, getting things wrong or looking a fool, but mistakes can open up all sorts of possibilities.

Also, most people tend to follow all of the rules and do what they are told.

You see, most of the time we do what we have always done and this results in us getting what we have always got. Even if we do things that others tell us to do, it doesn't mean that these are the best way or will get us the best results. It just means that worked for them, so you need to find what works for you.

## Mistakes are openings for ease

I have always been interested in finding easier ways to do things.

When I started in business my business advisor told me to write five letters a week and to send them out to businesses. I sent a few out, but soon got tired of the lack of response.

Maybe back then I wasn't as flexible in my approach. I did this for a week or two and then gave up and moved onto other things. I think I just wasn't sure how that was going to work and saw more pressing activities to attend to.

Two years into business I met with this business advisor again, to discuss another idea I had around business. He reminded me and told me again to send five letters a week to my ideal clients.

So not being one to avoid things twice I decided to get back into sending these letters.

In the first week I crafted a letter and sent five out to directors of organisations. I even stumbled upon an easier way to contact them by going through the Companies House website as their names, correspondence addresses and company information was all in one place.

One of the main difficulties in business is connecting with the people that you can help, connecting with potential customers and clients, and especially the decision makers.

My letters were sent and I made sure I put the contact details in my customer relationship management system with a follow up note. Then, three days later I followed up on the letters by giving them a call.

Copyright Natasha Davies 2016

First I spoke to a few receptionists. Then I spoke to a director and she said how lovely she thought it was that I had sent a letter and that she thought 'I like this lady already'. We spoke on the telephone for quite some time and arranged to meet.

We later met up for coffee and have spoken on social media since, too.

Week 2, I sent out five letters again to directors of companies. I was a little slower in following up but spoke to a few directors who said it wasn't something they were looking for right now.

Week 3, I adjusted my letter and put them in envelopes. I had written around three to directors and three to organisations.

Around five days later I started to ring to follow up. I asked, 'did you get my letter?'

Did you get my letter?

First I spoke to a P.A. who asked what sort of letter. I told her that it was a typed letter in a hand written envelope. She said she hadn't received it, but would ask the director if he had. She took my details to pass onto him.

The second person I spoke to was the receptionist at an organisation: 'no we haven't received that letter.' She gave me the director's direct email address.

The third one was another organisation: 'we haven't received your letter.' She took my details and said she would leave them on the manager's desk so he could contact me.

The fourth one: 'we haven't got your letter' .....

This went on. I apologised for the absence of my letter, we discussed where it could have gone and everyone was much more friendly and open. Some even started telling me that other things had gone missing and that maybe it was the mail service that was slow in delivering it.

One director emailed me back and asked if I could email the letter to him. When you are missing a letter you are curious to see what it said. After all people like certainty, they like to know and they aren't fond of uncertainty or not knowing.

Suddenly it hit me: did I actually post the letters? Maybe I didn't put any stamps on them? Were they still in my car?

However, I had got further and people were far more open in some respects when they hadn't received the letters. Suddenly I started questioning whether I needed to send letters at all, but just ring people up and ask them 'did you receive my letter?'

<u>When you notice, play around with it</u>

Being an experimental sort of person I picked up the phone and rang a few more people asking 'I'm just following up a letter I sent, did you get my letter?' I had some interesting conversations.

Again, people were more open and I got further, often getting past the gatekeeper - which can be difficult as we all know.

Then I thought to myself......What else did I not need to do?

You see, we are very good at following the rules yet we forget that really there aren't any rules; at any time we can break the rules, bend the rules or create our own rules.

So, if you are doing something and not getting far, take a step back and look at what you can drop from the process. We are so focussed on learning more or doing more that sometimes all it really takes is to do less.

Less is more, so to speak. If I don't send letters I save time and money. I don't have to buy stamps; I don't have to visit the post box.

I'm not really suggesting that you ring up people saying you sent letters when you haven't, but this mistake really illuminated for me that things get easier when you don't do something rather than when you do.

So, look at your processes and tasks and ask yourself what will happen if you don't do something? You may be surprised. Or forget to do things once in a while.

Often I forget to do things and other things show up. I forgot to email someone back, then found their email, shared their website, emailed them back and just as I did they text me.

We hadn't been in contact for quite some time.

A few days later I found the letters on the worktop in my kitchen, all sealed but never sent. The mistake of the missing letters was an amazing learning adventure. Mistakes are fantastic.

## **FINANCIAL FREEDOM IS A MINDSET AND YOU CAN HAVE IT RIGHT NOW**

Many people dream of financial freedom. To not have to worry about money and to have enough money to do the things that they want to do in order to enjoy life.

It's usually something they dream of achieving and something that they feel is not accessible to them yet. Therefore, they are already in a lack mindset around this issue.

It's something they want or need. It's always out of reach and something that they look forward to happening maybe one day in the future.

It's a dream, a wish, something they don't really believe is obtainable, but they hope.

Some are striving to create it and making good progress, but still don't have it. So, they are also in lack of financial freedom even though they are taking actions towards it, searching for the answer to find it. Yet, it eludes them and often they don't feel that they are as far along as they would like, not as successful as they would like or making enough money as they would like.

What people don't realise is that financial freedom has nothing to do with how much money you have and everything to do with your mindset around money.

It's not about the money

There are people with little or no money who are financially free, and people with more money than others can imagine who are in lack or believe 'it's not enough yet'.

It also has a lot to do with how you manage the money that you already have.

Many people spend money on things they don't need, but don't have budgets for the investments that could prove life changing for them.

They say they don't have enough but by someone else's standards they have plenty. It all comes down to how they think about the money they have and how they spend the money that they have.

When you have the right mindset financial freedom is something that you can experience right now, regardless of how much money you actually have.

## Think about what financial freedom means to you

- Maybe you won't have to work anymore?

- Not have to worry about money?

- Have enough to be comfortable?

Whatever it means to you there is someone else who has a completely different perspective.

Your mindset around money may get in the way of you following a dream that you would like to pursue. Many people feel locked in to a job they are not happy in, by the money that they receive.

## Attachment

Being financially free just means you have let go of any attachment to money, attachments to outcomes, anxiety and lack around the amount of money that you have.

When you manage the money that you have and prioritise the things that really matter to you, most people find that they have more than enough. Moving into abundance can help you to shift your perspective around money.

We put a lot of importance onto money and actually it's really just energy, just paper.

The meaning we give to it we can change at any time. How much we feel we need it we can change at any time and our thoughts around it we can change at any time. It doesn't have the power, you do.

What does financial freedom mean to you?

What will it feel like when you are financially free?

- Peace

- Freedom

- Happiness

These are a few emotions that may arise when you think in this way.

The thing is, even by thinking of being financially free you can experience these feelings right now and that works well, but involves some effort and practice on your part to create those thoughts and feelings.

Another way is to let go of lack and move into abundance. Again, this takes effort and practice and consciously repeating affirmations to open up to receiving abundance. Even if you do this, if you are still holding attachment it's an effort and with two opposing forces it can be a struggle.

Money has importance in our lives because we give it importance.

So much in our lives revolves around money; we give it power over us. We hear about our money story that holds us back, so we position ourselves as a slave to it and compare ourselves to others who may have more financial resources or material things.

You are being conditioned to consume

The media and advertising encourages us to base our self-worth around money. This is how we end up feeling like a nobody, because we don't have enough yet. This is how we are encouraged to strive, work hard and save.

I discovered a more permanent financial freedom when I was willing to let it go: to let go of striving, to not care anymore about money. To not base my success around how much money I was making, but more about the value I was creating and the difference I was making to people's lives. To let go of the outcomes and any attachment to money.

Copyright Natasha Davies 2016

The law of attraction states that if you want something you have to be willing to let it go. You have to release all attachment to it to attract it. Yet, most people are attached to needing more money.

What really struck me was that when I let go of this, all of the feelings I associated with financial freedom arrived. I was already doing what I loved. I stopped working, striving and started enjoying life. What also struck me was that synchronicity started appearing in my life.

Letting go

Things started showing up. Money started showing up. People started showing up. Opportunities started showing up, with no effort from me.

I was slowing down, doing less, being more me and enjoying life. I was going for walks, writing, reading and learning, which are all the things I love. I was writing this book. There was no rush, no urgency, no 'I should be working' once I had truly settled into this.

So, rather than waiting for financial freedom let go and all the feelings associated with it will arrive. And then, so will all the other things: the people, the money, the opportunities, the connections that will bring more abundance into your life.

When we are in lack of something or attached to it we repel it. Letting go of that attachment lets what we really want arrive. It's never really about more money, but what you think money will allow you to do, be and feel.

What are you waiting for?

Financial freedom can be yours at any time, when you let go of attachment to money, to outcomes, to lack.

Let go and find your own financial freedom right now.

## THINGS CAN BE EASY WHEN YOU BELIEVE THAT IS TRUE

I often hear comments like:

- 'Business is just so hard'

- 'I just have to be strong'

- 'I need to overcome it'

- 'If I can just get over this wall or hurdle'

These are common statements. They are all based on the belief that things are difficult. The majority of people think in this way and believe that where they focus their attention is truth. This, in turn, becomes their experience of the world.

What we focus on we get, right?

- 'We have to go through struggle'

- 'I love a challenge'

These are other examples of difficulty based beliefs. Even the statement that we are on a journey gives a linear explanation, with a start and end point which may not be necessarily the truth but more our representation.

## New meanings

Maybe it's an expansion, an opening, or a deepening of our understanding. We really need to question the description and find the one that best serves us. Just because the majority of people describe something in a particular way doesn't make it the only way.

Think for yourself!

The truly free minded individual knows that they can shift their focus and change their experience; that they can shift their focus to what they want instead; that they can create descriptions, meanings and understandings that serve them; that they can let go of any widely held meaning to find their own.

That changing their beliefs is the pathway to ease; that shifting their perspective opens new doors; and that changing the meaning makes things feel totally different.

## Blocks don't exist

What most people don't realise is that any block, wall or hurdle doesn't exist in reality, but only exists in thought. When you know this it frees you from the limitations that only really existed in your head.

That you are the one that created it and that you can change it, too. That someone else in the same situation would think differently.

The awakened individual might not necessarily think anything, but would let go of any outcome so that they are more open to the possibilities.

When we think we know the way something will happen we close ourselves down to the numerous possibilities of how that could actually show up.

So, moving back to things being difficult:

When we focus on difficult that's what we get. How would things be different if you held a belief that it was easy?

That there are a million and one ways that it could happen and you are open to them all. Wouldn't that feel light?

Someone said to me recently: 'It gets harder when you get older.'

Is that necessarily true?

What if they held a belief that it gets easier as you get older? I mean, you have more knowledge, more experience and you are wiser. Why wouldn't it get easier? Where is their focus? Are they focussing on their strengths?

Once they knew this they felt totally different.

Another example:

- Life is hard

What if you held a belief that life was a joy, a game, a party?

How would life be different then? If you don't want life to be hard you had better change that one quickly.

And another:

- 'It's difficult to find leads in business'

What if you had a belief that potential leads are everywhere, that you are a master of lead generation? Would your reality change? What new actions would you take? How would this free you up to reach out to people?

## Reflect who you really are

Often our beliefs aren't a true reflection of how things actually are. We may have built a belief or been handed down a belief that is no longer true; we have up-skilled but have not shifted our beliefs to match our reality, resulting in feeling unconfident.

When I was at school, I was in the second set for mathematics. I felt I wasn't good at this subject and so I developed the belief that I was not good at mathematics.

In later years I studied statistics, but still always said 'I'm not good at mathematics' and one day I reflected on this belief.

I concluded that this could not be true as I had studied statistics. I even pushed myself outside of my comfort zone in an effort to improve my skills in this area by completing an accountancy course.

Now I know that I didn't really need to prove anything, I simply had to reframe or upgrade my belief. 'I am great at mathematics, I am a statistician' wouldn't that have made all the difference. Or let go and just be me. Sometimes letting go is a whole lot easier. Why does it even matter?

## You always have the power

We are always able to instantly shift, reframe or create beliefs, but most people go on believing things that do not serve them. Most people are not even aware of what their beliefs are.

Becoming aware of your beliefs is the first step to ease. To freeing yourself. Then let them go, release them. Create a fantastic useful belief to take their place. This will feel uncomfortable at first, but stick with it and expand your comfort zone into new realities.

*Life is ease, joyous, amazing. Business flows to me in many ways. I attract prosperity and abundance. I am strong enough to know that being strong is not all there is.*

## Money story

We hear a lot about 'the money story', so what are your beliefs or your story around money?

We hear a lot about money blocks, but what if there were no money story and no money blocks? If you focus on blocks sure enough you will find them. What if money was just energy? It is thinking that makes it good or bad, right or wrong, difficult to obtain or easy to create.

So, use your imagination and create the thoughts and beliefs that will serve you; or let go of thought and be open to receive whatever opportunities appear to create money or whatever else you desire.

It's much easier to take action when your beliefs, thoughts and feelings support your goals and inspire you to move forwards; so play around with them, be present, let go and be open to receive.

- Life doesn't have to be difficult

- Business doesn't have to be difficult

- You can create ease, allow ease, and attract ease

But first you have to believe that ease is possible.

Do you?

# ENTREPRENEURSHIP CAN TAKE OVER YOUR LIFE – WHEN YOUR PASSION BECOMES YOUR PRISON

Starting out on the journey to build your dream can be thrilling, exciting and scary, all at the same time.

Often entrepreneurs can be so focussed on their goals that other parts of their life take a back seat and we often hear that entrepreneurs are trying to get more balance in their lives.

They may spend a lot of time working and not see their partners or families as much as they would like. They may spend a lot of time alone and not get to meet prospective partners or friends as much, either.

## Isolation

Entrepreneurship can actually be very isolating. Even though you may meet lots of people through your work, you may not get to meet people in a more relaxed environment where you are not in your work mode.

You may be outgoing at work but enjoy solitude at home, you can get used to that. I think that because entrepreneurs enjoy freedom this is another reason why they get used to solitude.

When you spend a lot of time alone you get to do whatever you want. You get to spend your time how you want to spend it. It's less complicated and you feel you have more control over your life.

However it is this control over your life that stops you from living it.

What if the part that takes a back seat is your life? What if you feel comfortable working 80 hours a week because you feel in control of that bit, but the meeting people, dating, spending time with your family you can't control because others are involved?

With all the working hard, striving, planning and goal setting entrepreneurs can sometimes forget to be present. Present in their life. Present in their families life.

Where is your focus?

What I mean by this is, that their focus is on their dream, their business, their customers and clients. They often forget about themselves. Their focus is out there rather than within.

Their focus is on creating the future, but they forget to live in the present. Have you ever felt like you were working hard but not getting anywhere? Going around in circles? This is why.

When you focus on a future and you are not there yet, forget to appreciate how far you have come or do not appreciate where you are right now, you are missing out on life. Missing out on happiness. Missing out on experiencing success right now.

You see, when you are striving you are saying I want to be somewhere else and I am not happy where I am. It's not good enough. When you are striving you have to always be somewhere else, somewhere further along.

Appreciate your journey

When you don't appreciate how far you have come, when you don't focus on your strengths, when you don't celebrate your wins you are not rewarding yourself.

You are not appreciating your efforts and you are not patting yourself on the back and saying well done to spur you on to keep going.

As soon as you appreciate where you are right now because that is good enough, you are good enough, you can slow down and you don't need to strive anymore. You can be present and enjoy your life.

When you slow down you start to notice how you are enjoying life; and not only that, but that all the feelings that you were striving to achieve show up, as I have previously mentioned.

You see - peace, happiness, joy and fulfilment can't show up if you are not being present. As soon as you start to be present they show up, as if by magic.

Most people never stop or slow down long enough to realise this. Slowing down feels uncomfortable, like you won't have time to get everything done, but time slows down when you do.

I urge you to lean into this discomfort, to expand your edges and your life.

Your life is too important to let it pass you by without truly living it. It's too important to strive it all away.

It's why many entrepreneurs and business owners work hard and then one day wake up to the fact that they aren't happy.

What are you striving for?

- Success

- Happiness

- Money

- Joy

- Peace

- Lifestyle

<u>Stop striving</u>

When you strive for success it eludes you. Even though in other people's eyes you may be successful, to you, you aren't successful enough yet.

When you strive for anything it eludes you because you are in lack, you don't have it yet, you need it so it will always be just out of reach.

How does that feel when the things you want you don't have? That may be what motivates you, but while you are motivated you are still striving your life away.

Being present means that you will enjoy your life more. If you are being in work mode at all then you are not being yourself. If you want to be in work mode and fit in, get yourself a job.

## Being free

Entrepreneurs are free, so be free by being yourself at work and at home. Have that consistency and authenticity running through your life and you will be happier.

To live authentically is to be yourself and to be present all of the time, regardless of what situation you are in.

When we try to achieve work-life balance or manage our time we are trying to control the situation. When we are present we are letting go of control and being more open to the possibilities. We are slowing down as we have nowhere to get to.

We sink more into who we are; we start to enjoy life in the moment. But how do I get anything done? I hear you say.

Getting things done is striving, so we have to let go of the idea of work in that sense. When we let go and are present things show up, because we show up differently. Our energy is different and this presents differently to others.

## Let yourself be drawn by the pull of what you love

Follow your soul and do what you love and it doesn't feel like work. Writing this book was a great experience; it was a joy.

Creating the time to write fed my soul. Come from that place and you will always be happy.

Other people start to react differently towards us. We get different results. People often think that to get different results you have to do something different, but you only have to show up different or be different to get different results.

When you show up other people do. Everything starts on the inside and affects the outside, not the other way around as most people imagine.

# THE FALLACY OF THE INNER SABOTEUR

We hear a lot about the little voice in our heads called the inner saboteur, but how do we know this actually exists? Are we just hypnotised into believing in it, because this is the commonly held belief? Psychology often refers to this separate entity controlling our thoughts.

I have a book at home called *The Inner Saboteur* that I bought some years ago and I certainly have at various times held a view that something was holding me back.

That saboteur is you

Then I realised that something was me. Then I discovered that I could quieten and, in fact, silence my inner saboteur with a number of techniques. Then I discovered that I could let the whole idea go altogether. It has no power, then.

Clients often come to me saying that they too feel there is something holding them back; or that part of them wants to do something and another part of them wants to do something else.

Often they have a little voice in their head that is negative and tells them that they can't do something, that there is no point trying or that they will fail.

Part of them wants to follow their dreams, while the other part wants them to stay safe and have security.

## Go deeper

When we go deeper the thing that is holding them back is always themselves. The parts that have this argument and keep them from moving forwards are actually parts of themselves, too; but it isn't the parts holding them back, it's the fact that they have this disagreement.

Going deeper again we find out that both parts actually want the same things, so why all the fighting?

It would be a lot easier if these parts could just get along. Accepting these parts as part of you is key. Aligning them together so they point in the same direction helps.

Accepting and letting go of them. Accepting you, all parts of you.

## Responsibility

So why would we give up control and responsibility to the so-called inner saboteur? Because that is exactly what we do when we believe in its existence.

It gives us an excuse not to step into our full power, not to be the best version of ourselves that we can be, not to achieve what we could have achieved.

The inner saboteur is a get out clause. Think about it; think about all the things that you can't do because of it. You see, I know that you can do these things, but believing in an inner saboteur isn't helping you to help yourself.

No saboteur = Action = Results

Someone inspired me to write this post. They were saying how they could not write what they wanted to write. They gave lots of reasons and one was the inner saboteur. I suggested that they slow down; they did and they wrote double what they wanted to write.

The inner saboteur was part of their story of can't. So, why do we hold onto this idea? I mean does it help us? Does it serve us? Does it take us closer to our goals or help us find ourselves more?

No, it keeps us safe and away from change.

Or, what we think is safe. What we don't realise is that nothing is static. Life is happening... change is happening. We cannot stop change and holding onto safety and comfort means we wait until we are forced into decisions, rather than consciously making decisions that serve us.

When we make our own decisions we feel liberated, we feel instantly better, just having decided or taking a few steps in the direction that we want to travel in. So, to feel better just step up and decide.

## Comfort

When we hold onto comfort we ensure discomfort, as we don't feel in control of our lives. This discomfort stays with us for the long term because we never move through it. When you choose uncertainty this only remains until you get used to the change, so actually pays off in the long term and gives you more comfort, builds your resilience and adds to your strengths.

So, back to the inner saboteur: he or she is your excuse to stay in comfort, to not experience failure, yet by default you fail because you never try. You never give it your best shot. You never step up into what you could fully achieve.

When you demand no excuses from yourself you have to wave goodbye to the notion of the inner saboteur. There is no room for him or her in this mindset.

Can you imagine the Navy Seals or the SAS saying 'I feel like I want to complete this mission, but part of me is holding myself back'? They have a no-excuses mindset. These forces just wouldn't work if they had an inner saboteur or believed in one.

So, the inner saboteur is not in everyone; it is only in us if we believe in the concept and if we allow it to be part of our reality.

It's actually you. Any voices in your head are you. When we believe in an inner saboteur we give up responsibility to it and that means we can't change it.

So, we need to stop believing in this separate entity, we need to stop giving it a name. We need to accept that it's us who are holding ourselves back; it's us who are arguing with ourselves in our heads. That it's us who can decide to stop and step into who we really are, so that we can achieve what we want to in life.

Because when you believe that nothing can hold you back except yourself, then you can find a way forward by allowing yourself to learn, to fail, to succeed and by letting go of what that might mean, as it's all a part of the process.

When you believe in the existence of the inner saboteur it allows you to feel ok about not doing what you want to do, because it's not your fault.

But, do you know what; this is a victim position where you have no control, which doesn't feel very good at all.

Let go of the inner saboteur, let go of anything that doesn't serve you to be the best that you can be.

You will achieve a lot more.

# HOW TO WRITE A BOOK, 1000 WORDS A DAY

As I wrote this book as part of a 1000 words a day challenge, I had to include some guidance about this so that you can do the same.

For as long as I can remember I've wanted to write a book. I think writing a book is on many other people's to-do list as one of the things they would like to do in their time on this earth. Whether it's a book about their life, their experiences or something that they feel will help others.

Writing will help you find many things

Writing is also an insightful activity for our own benefit, too. It helps you to reframe and make sense of experiences, find a way through trauma or create the future that you want to create in reality. To learn to let go, to create clarity and focus, and to develop a direction.

So, what stops people pursuing this dream? That will be the usual reasons: lack of time, lack of resources, you don't know what to write about, you don't have a title.

I always like to find easier ways to do things, as you may have noticed, so I've been creating easier ways to write a book. One idea was to work with other entrepreneurs and coaches to each write a chapter of a book.

The great thing about this idea is that we could all then share this finished book with our mailing lists and across our networks, reaching and inspiring more people. This would also raise all of our profiles.

The most effective and easiest way I have found to write a book by yourself is to write 1000 words a day consistently for a whole month or 31 days. Of course, you can do this for a longer or shorter period of time, depending on how long you want the book to be.

I created a challenge in one of my Facebook groups to do just this. Over the course of 31 days I created over 31,000 words in this way.

Many people get stuck on what to write, what the title would be or whether it would inspire them to write consistently. I had tried to write a book previously by starting with a topic and a title, and had lost motivation because I wasn't sure if it was a topic that really inspired me.

No Rules
------

In this challenge I decided to choose a different topic each day and to write about the topic that arose for me each day; a topic that inspired me, whatever that was.

I let it flow and had no preconceptions or rules.

I had no thoughts about how these topics would fit together, only a sense that some of them would and if I wrote enough of them I would soon have a sizeable book in my hands.

I wrote at different times of the day, but found that the most productive time was during the working day when I created the space to just write and to do nothing else.

I wrote 1000 words on each topic as a note on my Smartphone and used a word count app to check how many words I had written. Once completed, I emailed the note to my own email address, so that I could collate them and edit them later into book format. That took me only a few days.

Learning
--------

Thinking about the subject topic too much made it harder to write; not creating distraction free space made it harder to write. However, when I sat in a coffee shop with an hour to myself and the space to do nothing but write, this resulted in the words flowing easily.

Leaving it until very late to write made it feel more of a chore. I started to look forward to creating the space to just write; to have dedicated time to explore my thoughts and to feed my soul. I found it to be a very illuminating and insightful experience.

The more I wrote the better I got. I found I could write the first 500 words straight off without much thought. Then I would add the other 500 to complete the task.

I wrote while waiting for clients, as I always arrived early to appointments. I wrote while my son was in the bath; I would sit on a bench in the bathroom and write. I wrote in bed, I wrote in the car, I wrote in some beautiful places, but each day I wrote without fail even when I didn't feel much like writing.

My son was ill one weekend and I still wrote, even if it was 11pm I always completed before 12. I held myself accountable to what I said I would do each day.

I published a few pieces for my blog, as I did feel that while I was taking part in the challenge I wasn't paying my blog as much attention as usual.

## Keep going

There were days when it would have been easy to give up, to not write on that day, to say that I had too much happening in my life; but I always remembered it was only 1000 words, it was only 30-40 minutes and I had to create that time to make it happen. Each 1000 words was a step towards my 31,000 target and I really wanted to hit my target.

If I had given up on one day it would have been easy to give up on others too, and it was only for 31 days.

I did it and completed 31,000 words in 31 days and was congratulated by people who said how inspiring it was to watch me achieve my 1000 words consistently every day.

Even after the finish date I still wanted to make time to write every day. It's so soothing to the soul and I received some amazing gifts and insights while taking part in this challenge.

I learnt to slow down more than ever. I learnt to let go of striving and I found everything that I was looking for in that space. I also found other ways to create money with talents that I had forgotten that I had.

So what started out as a challenge to write 31,000 words in 31 days actually became the piece that I needed to have everything that I want in life.

To be present and to enjoy life in the moment right now. I was working hard, but striving, and it was during this challenge that I got my 'enough' moment. Writing helped me to slow down and really appreciate what was truly important.

I also had my book, at last.

So, that's one I can tick off my bucket list.

It's the book that you are reading right now. It doesn't take long or that much more effort to create something truly amazing. You just need to start and take consistent action.

It's also really easy to write the next one and the next one; I am definitely a writer now.

## SHOWING UP FOR YOUR BUSINESS AND YOUR LIFE

I had a cancellation this morning which was genuine, as the person really wanted to attend my group and had cancelled another appointment to be there. These things happen but it made me reflect on how many people don't show up and don't let people know.

Over the course of my business there were a lot of people that just never arrived, especially in the early days.

<u>I did things to change this</u>

They would say they were coming and then either not show up or something else would come up. People would book coaching appointments and just not turn up at my office or would talk themselves out of arriving.

People would say yes to being coached and then change their minds.

Back then I was, and have always been, someone who if I said I was going to do something I would do it - so I assumed others were like that, too. I soon learned that this was not the case.

So, I stopped making everyone an appointment and started qualifying people first.

## Mindset and tipping points

There is also a tipping point for showing up at events and meetings. So, it's how important it is to us and how our self-talk is around this.

'I don't really want to go.' 'I don't know who will be there.' 'I don't suppose I'll miss anything.'

But you do miss out on things and you don't even know what you are missing out on because you never showed up. It's all about focus. We tend to focus on what we know or what our experience has been and not the possibilities of the Unknown.

We don't just do this in business; we do this in life, too. So, if this is you, what opportunities are you missing out on if you never explore them by not showing up?

People who focus on the possibilities, e.g. 'The person I need to speak to might be there', ' I may meet a possible client there', 'there are all sorts of possibilities that could show up there' show up because their focus is on the Unknown, the possibilities and what might happen.

We get what we focus on, which is why people who focus on possibilities and show up tend to be luckier in business and life.

## I show up

Writing this book 1000 words a day also made me realise how much and how consistently I show up. When I make appointments I show up, when I plan groups and events I show up. When I'm writing 1000 words a day and I'm focussed on that, I show up. If I focussed on writing a book it would be overwhelming, a huge task and that would stop me from starting. I have shown up every day to write, without fail - even if I had to tweak it a little at the start by chunking down the task.

What drives me? I want to feel good. If I start making excuses, not doing what I said I would do, not showing up I will feel bad.

Most people stay with comfort. They imagine if they do these things it will be hard, difficult, they don't have the time. So their drive works the other way around keeping them where they are.

This is a simple shift to showing up. Finding the driver and turning it on, then using it till you get used to showing up to feel good.

When I got further into business I started learning to say no more to things that were not aligned. I was group leader of a network for 6 months then I stood down because I wanted to focus on my own business. I got asked to lead another group and I declined.

Showing up isn't about just arriving, being where you say you will be or letting people know when you can't make it.

<u>Saying no is showing up</u>

Saying no is important too and showing up doesn't mean showing up for everything. You can show up 100% of the time, but say yes and no to things, too. In fact, you need to show up to say no. I still think it's good business if you have to cancel to let people know, and lots of people do.

You can weigh up the options of how to spend your time, but before you say no to something consider this: you cannot weigh up the options of what might happen if you show up, if you are not focussing on the possibilities.

This requires using your imagination in a new way. Not to imagine how hard, difficult or a waste of your time something may be; but to imagine things that are outside of what you currently believe possible, to embrace the unknown, to let go of certainty and the need to know, to let go of control and go with the flow.

You never know, one day the person you didn't show up for may be on an interview panel for that job you want, or may be the owner of the house you want buy, or may be the person who holds the key decision to something that you really want. Stranger things have happened.

I heard a story recently of a woman who had been rejected for a job and had some pretty bad feedback from one man on the panel; basically, that day even though she showed up she didn't SHOW UP.

A few years later she had another interview for a speaking arrangement that she really wanted and had worked hard for; who should be on the panel, but the same man. Her heart sank. He had given her such damning feedback she really thought he was never going to give her the job.

So, she pulled it together and did the interview and she got the engagement. When it was over she asked the man if he remembered her. He said no, should he? She reminded him of that interview years ago and the feedback he had given.

He was astounded and said you are like a completely different person I never would have realised that was you.

Copyright Natasha Davies 2016

Her showing up had made all the difference.

- At any time you can decide to SHOW UP.

- At any time you can decide to shift and focus on the possibilities.

- At any time you can embrace the Unknown and see what happens.

When people do this that's when the magic starts to happen - in both business and life.

## ONE ACTION A DAY – BUILDING CONSISTENCY

It really doesn't matter what actions you take, you just need to take lots of them.

We get a little too hung up on taking the right actions, doing things the right way or not getting it wrong, but actually consistent action will bring results. Clarity and focus can help.

And failure can bring insights that can move you quickly up a level. I forgot to send my letters recently, which resulted in me finding a better way that saved me time money and effort. If I hadn't failed I would never have discovered that there was a better way.

Failure is how we learn, it's how we succeed, it's how we find a better way. Those who are afraid to fail never experience these things.

So, take action and fail occasionally. There is no failure, only feedback.

Post on social media, create videos, send letters, ring people, call into businesses, go networking, speak, do whatever you feel like doing.

Have fun with it. Provide value and enjoy giving, connecting with and meeting people. When we get in our heads about it all that's when it stops being fun and becomes hard work or something to stress about.

Reach out

Reach out to people in a happy way, leave people feeling good, light and touched by your connection.

Raise their vibration, raise your vibration. Don't waste time or energy on doubt. Don't take anything seriously, chase the no's, play around with your approach, and make it a game.

There are lots of ways that will help you to move forward with ease. You can't control your results or how many people connect with you, are interested in what you offer or sign up and use your services; all you can control is how much action you take and action = results.

So put your focus on that: taking action every day. Small actions build up to big results.

- Write and send one letter a day that's five a week

- Ring one person a day that's five a week

- Post one social media post in lots of groups on a day and this will add up too and build your following

- Visit one business a day and make an in-person connection

- Create a new offering a day, something that could give you passive income

- Write one blog a day - blogs are a great way to attract clients

- Give one business card out a day

- Meet one person a day for a business conversation or connect over coffee or Skype

It's these small actions that add up to results, but you have to do them consistently. It's these small actions every day that will connect you and the people that will benefit from what you can provide.

Some days you will find that you double up or even 10x your efforts.

Build on this idea and add new activities.

## Look after yourself

Remember to do things for yourself, too, like slowing down, maybe have a walk a day or listen to a podcast a day, read a few pages of a book a day.

Burnout isn't fun and I'm a firm believer in looking after yourself first. You are the centre of your business and without you it doesn't flow, so that's what you aim for: flow with a little stretch.

Do one thing that scares you each day and you will learn to make fear your friend. Through facing your fears you will have growth.

When I had a job I used this idea of chunking my housework into smaller parts. I was never really fond of these tasks, so I started cleaning one room a day or doing a few tasks each day - it made the job a whole lot easier and more enjoyable.

You can also chunk down other tasks. Have a pile of paperwork?

Deal with one piece a day. Need to de-clutter? Tackle one area a day.

DIY? Do one small job a day.

You will see progress.

See, when we set out to do things we tend to tackle it as a whole, meaning we can become overwhelmed and stuck.

Breaking it down and keeping it simple is a way to take action, have fun and get the job done, and then you get results.

Make use of time

Also when I worked in my job I would see how much I could get done for my business during my lunch hour.

Over the course of a few weeks I had accomplished an extraordinary amount of tasks, just by breaking it down and making it a challenge. So, in around a 40 minute lunch (I had to eat, too) I ticked many tasks off my list. My website took shape, I made posters, flyers, booked rooms, designed business cards and a whole lot more.

People use the excuse that they don't have the time, but we all have time - it's how we use that time. How do you use your lunch hour? Your evening? Your first hour in the morning?

I also joined the 5am club to create two hours twice a week to write all my essays for university. Having a 3 year old meant I didn't get the time to myself to do it and by the evening I was tired, so this way worked really well.

## Language

The language you use is important too, as to keep up the action and commitment you need to have no excuses.

When I said I would write today I mentioned writing when my son was in the bath OR when he goes to bed.

Even using the word 'or' wasn't a clear commitment and gave me a get out clause to leave it until later; and here I am, writing at quarter to 11, o we really have to watch and notice the words that we use. This can help us in being more committed.

- Using 'I will' instead of 'I might'

- Using 'I'm going all in' instead of 'I'll try'

- The word 'try' is one of the biggest precursors to lack of results

As Yoda says, 'there is no try only do or do not'.

So please let go of the word 'try', if you ever want to make a success of anything or commit to action. I don't think I ever use the word try, although I know many years ago things would have been different.

It takes training to change these things, it takes becoming aware of them and making a conscious choice to use different words, but after a bit of practice it becomes automatic and you really don't think about it anymore you just do it.

But you can always tackle one thing a day, too.

What one thing can you do consistently that will make all the difference?

# SLOW DOWN AND THINGS SHOW UP

When I chased them they eluded me - it was hard work.

I spent lots of money running around meeting people for coffees, going to different networks. So, I cancelled my network subscriptions and created my own network for women leaders.

These were coffee meet-ups and a mastermind group where leaders could connect, collaborate and create. I wanted to make space for others like myself to come together and create ease and leverage.

When I started I had no idea how this would work. I looked within and asked 'who would be my 10 out of 10 clients'? The answer came: 'leaders, women leaders', mainly because I was one.

Later this became Womenspire leaders, so women who inspire other women.

So, I found a great image and wrote two posts with the words:

**Are you a Womenspirer?**

**Are you a leader?**

**Do you want to create magic for women everywhere?**

Copyright Natasha Davies 2016

**I would love to connect with you.**

I had no idea the response would be so phenomenal or what would happen next.

170 women replied with 'yes that's who I am, I would love to connect with you.' They were women from countries across the globe.

<u>People like to belong to groups</u>

This is where I learnt to never be afraid to label people. People like to belong to groups. Having such a phenomenal response the fear kicked in and I said to myself...What do I do now?

I had no idea I would get this many responses and had nothing planned or created. It just started with me looking inside about who I really wanted to work with. I had no plan or vision about where this was going from there.

At this point I started connecting with these women through Skype, speaking to them and asking them what I could create for them.

I spoke to women all over the world: Switzerland, USA, Ireland, Denmark, France, U.K. and many more countries. I spoke with them, about how I always felt there was something missing in networking events for me. Many agreed. After a while I was overwhelmed as the yesses just kept coming.

I thought to myself, 'what do I do, this is quite time consuming for them and me, spending an hour with each person?'

Seeing through the story

Then it occurred to me: I could do a webinar. But, I'd never done a webinar. Well, I had once but it had gone really wrong.

I struggled with this for a few minutes.

My next thought was... 'Why can't I do a webinar?'

I got to work, signed up for Google hangouts then realised I could only have 10 other people on there. I needed something bigger.

I found some webinar software with a free trial and signed up. I scheduled one to invite the rest of the Womenspirers to. Then I practiced and carried out a few test webinars with myself, built a welcome page and played around with it until it worked.

The webinar went well and some asked when I was doing another one. I still had women asking to connect 1-2-1. So I started an online group for everyone to join.

Then I joined Meetup and started a local Meetup group.... then two, then three. They filled up quickly and we had around seven at the first meeting, which went well. When I worked on the structure I realised that if I was going to make this work I had to create a membership group.

Structure

So, at the next meeting I discussed structure and my idea of creating a membership group. We had met for coffee twice, but as soon as I mentioned an investment every month there were some questions and stories.

I was used to this when I talked about commitment and money.

People said they wanted to see what they would get, so I figured that I needed to step up so that they might. So, I booked a room and launched my group.

Many that had brought up objections did not turn up and on the day we had three people. I did my presentation, we had some discussion around international woman's day and a speaker from the group and at the end I told them how it was going to work. The investment and the fact that today it was almost half price.

The objections started again. Can we have three hours, can't we just meet for a coffee. I had decided after the last meeting that maybe some of these women were not right for this particular group of higher level action takers. Energetically they just weren't there yet. So I said no, this is how it works and it isn't going to be for everyone.

One lady signed up and we booked a room to start the following month. I decided that it would be a mastermind group of high level action taking leaders and many of these women didn't fall into this category.

I have continued the coffee groups for those who aren't ready to take action and collaborate yet as part of the mastermind group.

I invited another lady along who I felt was a good fit, then a few more.

In our online group I started connecting members with each other and collaborating with them too online and offline.

The online group now has over 100 members from across the globe. All women; inspiring other women. The group has no advertising so people share inspiring posts and ask for what they need so that we can all assist each other.

The collaborations have been fantastic too. As it's a creative space members have come up with some amazing projects.

All the Meetup groups will now become masterminds at £42 a month. So, smaller groups with quality not quantity.

Some members have shown an interest in starting their own groups in other areas as luminaries, so that they get free membership and give two hours of their time every month to run a group.

Meaning they get to spend time around other Womenspire leaders and collaborate on projects as well as inspire other women.

The groups are creative spaces. To connect, collaborate and create. Create leverage and ease. If we want to do something we can now collaborate and do it together to create ease.

They are still building, evolving and forming, but are full of amazing Womenspirers.

# DEFINING YOUR OWN SUCCESS

When I started out in business I wanted to create the largest coaching and training business in my country.

That's a big goal, but I figured you need to aim high. I got an office, a computer and some furniture, put my ad in the local services and waited for the phone to ring. It didn't.

This is when the striving and hard work started. I got out there and networked. I leafleted, I spoke, and I telephoned, wrote letters and basically got really busy. I worked hard to build my social media presence and was posting night and day about how I could help people through coaching.

I worked with clients, I ran workshops, and I facilitated training. I ran 40 workshops for a government organisation and 25 workshops in one month.

I was fast, overcame all the challenges that came my way and had a lot of growth. I learnt a lot about myself and found out who I was. I became who I needed to be to make it work.

I started lots of projects, had lots of ideas, I created the Womenspire leaders network with an online group and some Meetup groups and started to turn these into membership groups; again, I came across challenges and stepped up and overcame them.

Recently I have started writing and slowing down and creating time for this. Opening up this space and slowing down has made me realise a few things.

1. My life is consumed by the business of coaching
2. This is not why I became a coach
3. I'm tired of striving
4. I've been running from myself

I have fallen into the trap of thinking that to be of value I have to create big things. That I am not enough. I've been chasing success, but attributing that success to the amount I have in my bank account.

I mean, that's how we measure business success, isn't it?

Define your own success

How many connections we have, how much revenue we make, how many clients we serve.

I have realised that this is all bullshit. That this may be how most people measure success, but I am not most people so I needed to stop, slow down and re-evaluate what success means to me.

Being constantly striving, always being in a rush and not appreciating or enjoying life where I am is not success.

Slowing down, creating space to enjoy the things that I like to do; slowing down and creating deeper more meaningful connections, and really serving people on a daily basis whoever I meet. That is success.

Having time for me is success and letting go of all of this pointless striving.

So I decided to let go and slow down.

I realised that I don't need to go big to create the best coaching and training business in my country, I realised I didn't even care about that. I wanted to create the best coaching experience for my clients, one at a time.

So, this brings me back to my focus and goals. I just need to work with 15 clients. I need to stop running around everywhere and sit still.

I need to delve deep into my own soul; my own passions, my own peace and people will show up.

I've been focussed on helping others so much and I'm letting go of that, too. I'm letting go of coaching. I'm letting go of the business of coaching and what I think that looks like.

## Show up

I'm going to show up and serve people powerfully instead.

I'm going to live my life first, though. I'm going to be happy and spend time on things that I enjoy. When you are striving you are trying to look relaxed, but you aren't really relaxed.

I have been looking at some coaches and thinking, 'wow that looks like hard work.' Now I realise it's because it is.

You don't have to be earning six figures to change someone's life. You don't have to have a huge successful business - you just have to serve the person in front of you deeply.

Phew! All that took a lot of energy. Now I feel at peace, now this feels easy. Now I can enjoy more of life while serving those people too.

## Authentic living

Coaches talk a lot about authenticity, but when you are striving to show the world you are happy, when actually you just haven't noticed yet that life is slipping by.... that's not authentic. You need to be truly living the life you portray for yourself first and foremost, for your family and for your clients.

You can only do this by slowing down and living in the moment. This is hard for most people as we have all been taught that work is hard, work is long hours, work is tough etc.

There is no work, only creating and enjoying a life where you are happy and living it. Not in the future, but now.

When we chase we repel things, when we sit they come to us. This is how things work.

Be you, share the lessons, and share the love and what you want will see the value that you can provide, not because you say it but because you live it. Many coaches that I have spoken to aren't living by what they preach.

I always wondered why every time I said I was at a luxurious hotel people contacted me.

Because I was living what they wanted, being what they wanted to be.

Most people aren't being present; most people aren't happy with their lives; most people want more but don't know how to get it.

Most people aren't happy with themselves. Most people hate their lives and their jobs. When I worked in a factory, when I left, when I studied, when I started a business, people weren't happy for me because they wanted what I had. I had forgotten this one simple truth.

Be happy it makes people envious.

But, it makes you happy.

And being happy is all there is in life. It's the most wanted possession, except people don't realise it's always within their grasp if they just allow it.

## MY MIRACLE

I had my miracle and I cried..........

Tears of joy, of course.

All of a sudden I felt like I'd been on some kind of focussed train, in a tunnel heading fast in one direction, afraid to stop at stations for too long for fear of being held back; because I needed to get somewhere and away from where I was right then.

I was measuring my success with other people's rulers. I was striving for freedom and happiness while slowing down and enjoying snippets of my life.

While the freedom and happiness was right under my nose, but I was going too fast to notice. When a part of your life becomes so consuming it takes over and you miss the most important moments: the NOW.

### Obsession

Whether it's work, business or a relationship, obsession sends you on a one way train to the destruction of all you have created.

Control was at the heart of this journey. It may not have looked like it from the outside, but from where I'm now looking I can see it plain as day.

It kept me safe; I thought I could control everything, when really I didn't need to: control was the thing that was keeping me exactly where I was. It kept me on the hamster wheel and one day it just hit me. I might as well just go get a job. I was happier in a job.

I got into business so that I could help people more, and so that I could enjoy more freedom and autonomy, but the very thing I had created kept me caged.

My days were stressful, busy and long. And although there were times where I didn't work hard, in my mind I was so focussed that I was working 24/7. Everything revolved around coaching and business. Who I was became 'The coach'; it was my identity.

I had worked so hard becoming who I needed to become, I had lost who Natasha was.

Natasha was fun and playful, always smiling; she was present and enjoyed life; the coach was focussed, driven, serving, needy and wanting to share the growth and journey that she had experienced.

It was an amazing journey, but what strikes me is that it's a journey that has taken me full circle to where I started before all the bad shit happened.

Before being cheated on, lied to; before being a victim of domestic abuse; before all the not very satisfying relationships; before the confusion and wondering who I was; before all the wanting more for myself; before all the self-development.

Awake

I was back to square one, but freer, cleaner, fully aware and awake.

Have you ever wondered what it would be like if you could go back to being 18, knowing what you know now?

That kind of describes how I feel, hence the tears of joy.

It's been a hard journey, it's been an interesting journey, but the shifting point for me was when I let go of the journey, got off the train, sat on the platform and started to just enjoy where I was right now, there and then.

It was hard at first. That journey had been my life for the past two years and started before I started my business. Letting go sounds easy, but it takes both practice and faith. It also took some pain and the 'I've had enough of this' moment.

So I started to let go. I decided to spend a few days just doing nothing but enjoying life. And this was a revelation.

I started to realise that when I started out in business and when I was on that train, the life I was experiencing by slowing down was exactly the life I was striving for, and all I had to do to enjoy it was to stop and let go.

For all the advertising and posting on social media, for all the speaking and networking there were only a few areas where my clients had approached me. All the rest was me just thinking I had to be busy.

Filling up every moment, so I would be busy and could justify this journey of entrepreneurship to others. Why did I have to justify it to anyone?

Don't create a job

When we start on this road we have to be careful that we don't just create another job. If we left our jobs to be more autonomous and help people more, then that should be our focus.

This was indeed my focus when I started out, but then I hit the ground running and haven't stopped. I obviously paused and was present with all of my clients, but then off I went again.

I was afraid to stop; I was afraid to slow down too much so when I did it was only to rest, be creative then take action.

What I've learnt from letting go of the striving is that instead of thinking of a big vision of somewhere to get to, I need to serve one person at a time, and that starts with me.

So, I've decided to redefine business. When I run my business I also want to walk my dog, write, meet friends, read, clean my house, be with my children and have time alone which doesn't mean being at work.

I'm still only working with 15 one-to-one clients. I'm going to be running my Womenspire leaders groups, but giving them more time to naturally grow and evolve. I've slowed down on social media and realised that I post much deeper insights when I do less and just enjoy life.

This is living, this is being present in my own life; business is part of that, but it's also part of being present in my own life, so now there is no business-only life.

There is being Natasha, enjoying life and serving the person in front of me. Sometimes that will be a client, sometimes it will be someone I just share a conversation with in the street and say 'wow that's an awesome pair of shoes' or ' have you ever tried letting go and slowing down its ace!'

This does not fit society's definition of business and that's ok, because society's definition of business didn't fit for me either.

What are you chasing? What is your definition of business?

# HOW TO CREATE A POWERFUL CONNECTION

I remember some years ago attending a group where we had a presentation on the hero's journey.

I was struggling with my relationship at the time and trying to understand the confusion I was feeling. I was also heavily pregnant with my second son.

We learned about the hero's journey and how it was an integral part of most stories and films, and then we were asked to write our own hero's journey.

Of course my relationship at the time came up and I related to this in my story.

There was a man sat next to me in the group who some years later I reconnected with and we met to talk about coaching.

He mentioned that when we met in that group he had thought that it was incredible how I had walked into a group of people that I didn't know and could be so open and vulnerable about my struggles and reflect on them in this way.

On other occasions I would be delivering training in my previous job and the comment that would often come up would be 'my psychiatrist told me I will be like this forever' - this was quite common in my line of work. I asked simply: 'how do they know? Is that just their opinion or a fact?'

Around a year or so later one person from my previous job had tracked me down and become a coaching client. They said they had looked for me for a year and always remembered what I had told them. Again, I had created connection.

What is creating a connection and how do you do it?

Quite clearly from the above examples, being vulnerable and speaking your truth is involved, but also being present. The more you learn and grow yourself, the more you are aware and awake and in a better position to create connection with others.

I had to know that psychiatrists can't read the future. I had to say something different than most people, as plenty of others just don't question these things at all.

In the first example I had to be open, honest, reflective and courageous, and not worry what others might think. To be able to do this in a room full of strangers you must be self-aware.

It's really just about you being yourself, but being yourself is a little ambiguous.

Yourself before thought, yourself before conditioning and beliefs - this equates to presence and an inner peace.

Then you exude a stillness, a sparkle, an openness. It also helps to embrace silence and space and not feel that you have to fill every moment.

<u>Be yourself</u>

Being yourself, courageous, vulnerable, honest and open is connection making gold dust. Especially in a world where most people are not being themselves at all.

The intention always being for the other person, whatever that may mean. Being of service to them, even if that means saying no or something they may not initially like.

The truth may piss you off, but then it will set you free.

All of this aside, I also think we should not be trying to create a connection with everyone we meet or see everyone as a potential client.

This is where coaches can give too much or become needy. If people aren't ready it's respectful to them to let them find their own way, and also respectful to yourself.

You can serve them with resources or by pointing them towards your online offerings or social media pages where they can get inspiration instead.

You hear coaches saying to just be you and be in service, but what I find is that if you are in service to everyone you get burnt out. And as you often don't get paid you aren't being in service to you.

After a while you won't be able to help anyone if you're not around anymore.

I've been thinking recently about some of the things we do as coaches that do not help us in business.

The scarcity principle

We are often too available to everyone, when we should be most available to those who are ready to do the work.

We meet other people's needs

When I first started out in business I would be driving all over the place meeting prospective clients, seeing them out of hours, stretching myself in all ways.

I would fit them in at the earliest opportunity, often moving other things. Many of these clients didn't sign up for coaching or weren't ready at the time.

It's better to ask them to come to you. To ask that they fill in a questionnaire or complete a task before you meet. The ones that are ready and serious will do so; the ones that are not won't.

As coaches we are not responsible for our client's lives, they are. People who are ready to be coached know this. So, why do we feel we have to help everyone? That we have to market to everyone?

Something I got clear on is who my clients are and where I can find them.

Where should I be marketing my services?

Which marketing creates coaching clients and which marketing doesn't create any but just takes up a lot of my time.

When we give lots away for free and are so readily available we devalue what we offer.

So, create connections only with people who will be most likely to become your clients.

Then, once you have a full and successful coaching practice you may want to create some pro-bono workshops for those who can't afford to sign up.

This makes far more business sense than continuously giving to people who aren't ready to receive yet.

Dating is a lot like coaching

If this was a romantic relationship would you try to have a relationship with someone who wasn't ready to commit?

Also, you may well have experienced that this kind of one sided relationship does not work and often leads to painful experiences.

I remember years ago reading an article on giving too much and creating space to beckon, not chase in relationships; I'm starting to notice some similarities with the coaching relationship between coaches and potential clients, too.

In dating I qualify prospects as to their level of commitment to a relationship and, quite frankly, when it says on their profile that they're not looking for any kind of commitment, where once I might have tried to convince them I now know to find someone who is ready for that. Coaching is much the same.

## WHAT'S SO AWFUL ABOUT BEING WHERE YOU ARE?

When you look at how far you have come you can appreciate your journey much, much more.

Most people are moving too fast and not creating space to do this self-reflection. To notice how detrimental not enjoying where they are is to their life and business.

We really need to slow down or life will pass us by. We really need to take stock of whether this is any sort of life at all.

We also need to switch off our handheld devices often and experience real life right now, in the moment.

We may want to be a six figure earner or a blogger or a retreat running coach, and we might want to get there yesterday . . . but we also want to get there alive and we want to have a good time getting there.

Enjoy every moment and then you'll enjoy life, whether you get to your goal or not. Actually letting go of the end result and enjoying the now can help you to reach it.

When you become more present, happier and more content then you become more of a magnet to those who are not.

They wonder what you have been drinking and they want some.

## Be congruent

What I realised was that I was teaching my clients things that I wasn't practicing myself. I have also heard many coaches say the same thing. We teach people to be present and live in the moment, but we ourselves are striving.

Or, I tell my clients to do things but I'm not doing them myself.

Do you think that looks hard or easy to our clients? Is that going to attract them or repel them?

As coaches we need to practice what we preach first, this is authenticity at its upmost.

Yes we are human, yes we fall down and we get back up, but being present should be the single most important factor because we have lives too and we need to live them, just as our clients do.

We need to be examples of living life to the full, of enjoying every moment and of living in peace with ourselves.

## Be happy where you are

We need to be happy with where we are right now, not striving for seven figures or a full coaching practice. If we slow down, be present and really enjoy life instead of just saying we are, I'm guessing all the things that we want will show up mainly because we have.

Right now, in the present moment, totally and fully, happy and content and in our hearts for ourselves and others.

# **SLOWING DOWN IN COACHING**

Right now I feel as though I have been striving for too long, as though I've been chasing a dream and going around in circles.

Yes, I have wins where I move forwards in my goal, but they are short lived and the work is hard.

I love to serve people and when I do it's an amazing feeling, but a lot of the work around coaching isn't serving: it's prospecting, it's attracting and to me this just feels needy, so I'm starting to question its usefulness.

In all this work I had forgotten to be me. In all this work I have been helping others to find themselves and live their lives, but have not been living my own completely.

I have been so totally focussed on my coaching business that my own life has taken a back seat and I am not content with this.

Balance

Before I was a coach I had balance: I went to work, did my job, came home and enjoyed life, the people around me and the weekends. I had stability and knew where I was. I had a regular income and guaranteed clients every day.

## Systems

These systems that bring a stream of clients to the door always seem to focus on there being a problem and a solution.

I know this is how marketing works, but I've avoided this because I don't think there are any problems - only human experience. But then, I am aware of this; many are not. Of course when you tell people they don't have a problem their pain goes away, which isn't that good for business.

I started focussing more on the people who are seeking pleasure, not the fixing of a problem.

When you focus on your dreams your problems disappear, but people often struggle with this. They need support; they are the action takers out there, doing it on their own.

They need support to be around positive influences: the pain is that they might fail, the pleasure is success. These people are me.

I realised I was at the point where I was only existing, while teaching others to live. My personal life had lost its importance and been taken over by my business. I wonder how many others feel this, too.

Sometimes I found myself choosing between my sick toddler and an event, because I didn't know who would be there and maybe there would be someone who could use my services. Work always won and my son would go to my mother's. This is not how I wanted to live.

The funny thing is that the realisation of this really helped me to focus on me and I felt stronger and more me than ever; it's just the personal fun and enjoyment part that now needs to happen, too.

I enjoy my work and helping others so much, but I got a little lost in it, in my mission. We can all get a little lost in our passions sometimes.

I need to let go of a lot of the striving to make room for fun. I need to let go of the chasing to make room for enjoyment and I need to slow down and enjoy the peace and tranquillity of just being. I'm sure this has helped you, too.

Now that I have noticed all this here is what I am doing about it.

I will continue to serve my current clients; however, I'm taking a step back from the business side of coaching and re-evaluating my life, my practice and the way I find the clients that I can serve.

I'm putting on the brakes, slowing down and noticing what's going on around me.

I want to spend more time writing and being in environments that are social and positive. I want to meet more interesting people and have more enjoyable experiences.

Getting out there

So, I've joined a few meet up groups, signed up for some events, and I've cancelled my business networking - I'm fed up of selling and doing my elevator pitch at networking events. I'm going to slow down and serve those around me, and myself.

We have all heard the saying that if everyone is doing it you should do something else. So, I'm only going to do it my way and a way that means I can enjoy my life, too. Are you following the crowd or blazing your own trail?

I'm getting off the business train and jumping on the train of enjoying my life. I'm stopping the business networking and starting to get to know people more deeply. I'm slowing down to connect more fully.

I'm letting go of the striving, the selling, the prospecting and I'm going to sit in a hotel lobby, have a coffee and write, just because I want to.

## Slow down and people show up

A while ago I did this and a man who ran 50 depots of a company sat down next to me and we had a conversation. I feel this works better, it serves people better and it serves me better. Because it feeds my soul and because we only get one life and we need to live it. Slowing down creates connection.

You see, what mostly attracts people to my coaching is when I speak and talk about my life. When they see me enjoying my life. When they see how open and vulnerable I can be.

When they see how nothing bothers me and how I navigate my way through life learning from my experiences. People want freedom, people want to feel good and people want to live. People don't want striving, it's hard work. People want ease.

They might think they want money, fast cars and nice houses, but it's because they think those things will bring them happiness.

## Happiness is always there

Happiness is actually right under your nose, but you are too busy striving for those things to see it. Connection is right under your nose, but you are in such a rush you miss it. If you always have to be somewhere else, you never get to experience the moment.

The beautiful deepness of each moment that's in front of you, right now. The depth of people's experience and character, the presence of their pain or happiness. The presence of your own pain or happiness that tells you that you are a human being and are truly alive.

# **NAVIGATING THROUGH CHANGE**

Whether it's change in personal lives or change at work or in business.

Things like:

- Relationship breakdown

- Loss of a loved one

- Children growing up and leaving home

- Retirement

Or

- Restructures

- Changes in employment or roles

- Promotions

- Redundancy

- The leap into entrepreneurship

- Stepping down from your successful business

These are all transition periods in life and all have periods of change and uncertainty. They all involve embracing the new and letting go of what was.

They often require finding a new identity and are often stressful periods in people's lives.

## Uncertainty

Most people don't like uncertainty or not knowing, and have uncomfortable feelings around these times. However, it's all a matter of perception, resilience and ability to trust yourself and the process of change.

When we resist our thoughts around it cause us pain and stress. When we try to understand it we are at a loss. Many people's health and wellbeing suffer in times of change. Often because they feel they have no control over the situation.

When we find new ways to perceive it and understand the process of change we learn to navigate it in a totally new way.

## Change and uncertainty bring gifts

They bring growth, new skills, new opportunities and learning to be comfortable and to navigate your way through change in a way that serves you, that makes all the difference.

- Understanding the process

- Focussing on your strength

- Creating the space to find a new identity

- To explore different perspectives

These can all help you to look after yourself better at times of change, or to gain clarity on your direction, to know yourself and what you really want and to feel more in control by focussing on what you can change rather than on what you feel you have no control over.

Change is always happening, but it's how we navigate and perceive it that makes the difference.

There are always gifts in everything and change means more possibility if you focus on that.

# THE CLIENT PROCESS

<u>Kindness service</u>

Be in service to people all of the time. Kindness is something that is rare today, as everyone is in such a rush. Slow down and be of service. I once stopped and chatted to a lady in a shop.

Say things to really serve them. She said you must help a lot of people, you are so kind. She was very curious. Create curiosity.

I asked a woman who was taking a picture of herself on a bridge if she wanted me to take her picture. At first she looked suspicious, then after I had handed her camera back she got really curious, asking me why I was here. Be kind and of service.

Be kind to yourself so that you can be kind to others.

<u>Consistent attraction/marketing</u>

Show up! Many of my clients say they kept seeing my posts and they liked my philosophy. Then, one day they had seen so many that they showed up and contacted me. Show up! Then your clients will, too.

Show up for yourself so that you can show up for others.

Letters

I send five letters a week to ideal clients just asking for connection, maybe an interview, and when I get a meeting I show up powerfully and serve. Focus on presence and connection.

Write for yourself so that you can write for others: journal daily to practice your writing and also to check how far you have come.

Attraction social media marketing can often look and feel desperate if done in a sales needy way.

Again, be kind and be of service. Be consistent. Be open and honest. Many of my blog posts have also prompted people to contact me. Another place where clients have been attracted to my message is public speaking. When I have had the opportunity to speak at networking and events someone usually asks to have conversation.

Be attractive! Live life

Touch your own soul so that you can touch the soul of others. Do the inner work so that you can help others to do that too. You can only take people as deep and as far as you have been yourself.

## Client creation

I talk to strangers. I'm curious, kind and deeply interested. I say what others will not. Truthful, honest and I listen. Be in service. Point out things they haven't noticed or aren't aware of.

Talk kindly to yourself so that you can talk kindly to others.

## Contact

People tend to contact me either through my website, on social media or in person, via events where I have spoken.

Occasionally I get a telephone enquiry. I may get a response to letters or a conversation I've had. I send them out a questionnaire and then invite them to a conversation at my office.

Slow down so that you can slow others down too. They need it more than they realise. People who contact you may be in a rush. Slow them down, they will thank you for it.

## Questionnaire

All new clients are required to complete a questionnaire before I will meet with them. I find that those that complete this questionnaire are more ready for coaching.

I have criteria for my 10 out of 10 clients so that I can notice when they contact me. I also regularly reach out to these people.

Do the work so that others are willing to do the work too.

## Telephone

Once a questionnaire has been completed and returned I will contact them by telephone to discuss this and to offer a conversation if they are ready for coaching. If not I will send them resources or invite them into one of my groups.

Listen to yourself, your heart and your soul so that you can listen deeply to others. No coaching yet! Invite them to a powerful conversation.

## Meeting

Meetings are either at my office or via Skype, depending on their location; I do not do coffee shop meets. Conversations last around 90 minutes. Ask for their permission to coach them. Be present and serve them in a powerful conversation. Slow down and be curious, coach deeper - one big insight is better than many small ones.

## Proposal

Depending on the course of the conversation I may offer a proposal - usually when they ask me how it works - and depending on whether I feel we are a good fit. If we are not a good fit I will explain why; if we are I sometimes test their commitment as I want to know that they are willing to commit the time, energy and money to the programme.

## Yes or No

If they are a yes I will ask for commitment and send them a proposal. A deposit or the full fees may be paid before the date of our first conversation. We will make a date for this. Fees are usually paid upfront before coaching begins.

If the conversation comes to an end and they haven't asked, I may ask them to a second conversation - depending on whether I feel they are almost ready or an ideal client. If it's a maybe or a no then we will part ways.

## Proposal sent

If a proposal has been sent but no payment I will follow it up by inviting them back for another conversation and serve them again.

## Starting coaching

We will discuss commitments and agreements of both parties. Make notes and type these up.

- Slow down and show up more powerfully

- Move them beyond what is comfortable

- Invite them to stretch what they thought was possible for them.

- Check in with them on their goals and direction.

- Ask for feedback on their coaching experience

- Send them resources

- Ask them what they need

- Ask them how you can serve them more fully

## Coaching form

One of their commitments is to fill in a coaching form before each session and to return this to me 24 hours before. If they don't I hold them accountable. Step up and they will too. Remind them of their achievements as you go along the coaching programme.

## Seeding

Throughout the programme remind them that personal development is a life long journey and ask them what else they want to work on.

## Re-enrolment

Towards the end of the programme ask them what their next big dream is. Offer to help with that.

All of this serves them to step up. We coaches have to lead, even though I always ask clients to lead the focus of each session.

## WHAT HAVE BEEN THE MOST DEFINING MOMENTS OF YOUR LIFE SO FAR?

When did you learn the greatest lessons? When did you make your biggest achievements? How did you feel? Of course, it's not all about hard work and achieving, maybe you learnt to let something go, to not worry about what others thought of you, to let things slide, to be easier on yourself or to take one day at a time and be present.

Life defining moments also aren't just about you. Maybe you learnt to get along with others more or to contribute more. Maybe your children taught you to be patient or your friends taught you to have fun.

Lessons can prompt us to either open ourselves up or close ourselves down

Did you learn from a painful relationship to close down your heart, trust and faith in people? Did you learn from a painful fallout with friends or family to have fewer friends?

Many people have negative experiences and live less because of them, while others have learnt to open up, even after closing down after painful experiences; we can learn to open up by learning to be vulnerable, going outside of comfort and learning to let the right people in.

Not everyone deserves a seat at your table and people have their own path to walk. Not everyone is meant to go with you on your journey for the whole distance

We are constantly learning and life defining moments are always showing up, all you have to do is be aware for and open to them.

Often lessons show up again and again until we learn the lesson or receive the gift.

Pain is inevitable; suffering is optional

These moments are often coupled with pain, anguish and struggle, but even this comes from our thoughts and how we perceive them.

If we see and receive the gifts then they become easier and we can turn these moments into learning experiences much more quickly than if we get stuck in the thought.

Here are 10 questions to learn from the burn:

1. Ask yourself, does it have to be this way? Is it just the way I am viewing the situation?

2. How would someone else view the situation?

3. What do I need to let go of?

Copyright Natasha Davies 2016

4. Or do I need to step up?

5. Which parts of this are my responsibility and which parts am I unnecessarily taking responsibility for?

6. Check in with your intuition if this situation is where you should really be right now

7. What will I gain and lose by staying in the situation?

8. What will I gain and lose by changing the situation?

9. What is the most powerful thing that I can do right now?

10. What is the gift or lesson I need to take away?

We can either be angry, frustrated, upset or thankful for the lesson.

Sometimes you will even be angry at yourself, but there are no mistakes, no stupidity, no foolishness - there is just your journey, feedback, lessons, awareness and growth.

<u>See the gifts</u>

Be kind to yourself and learn to let that go and enjoy the gifts. There are always gifts in everything.

As you learn to receive them your life will expand, you will grow, life will become more joyful and you will have lots more stories of life defining moments to share.

## BUSINESS – TOO MANY COFFEES

If prospects aren't qualified ideal clients why would you meet them?

On the hope they might know someone else or refer other work?

Stop playing small!

Make appointments only with your ideal prospects. Qualify your leads. Step into your greatness. Save time and energy. Time is money. Time is your life. Your time is precious, start treating it that way and others will too.

Serve the people you can help the most; serve the people who are ready to move towards you, because they know they have to do the work and are willing to do it.

Stop looking for help. Become a producer, not a consumer. I developed my own network, wrote my own book and created my own online packages for this reason.

Step up!

Plot the steps, sign up one person, take the first step and then the next.

Most people have a dream;

Some people have a plan;

The majority never fully execute.

Reach out to potential clients with an offer or a call to action, a conversation, and the benefits that they are looking for: increased profits, more time or whatever it is that they want and that you can help them with.

What do they want?

Do your research. Check out their website and their social media accounts. Google them.

Find out how you can serve them the most.

# WHERE TO FIND CLIENTS

When you know who your clients are and have clarity on this where do you find them?

This especially seems to be a question people ask about high ticket coaching. Where do you find the clients who will invest large coaching fees?

When I started in business my business advisor told me to send out five letters a week to businesses. To me this seemed too simple, but I thought I would try it and I sent out around 15 letters to organisations. After following these up and running into challenges where people said things like 'we already use coaching' or 'sorry we are not interested' or my not being able to speak to the decision maker I gave up on this method.

I had no idea at the time who my ideal client was or what I could provide which didn't help. I spoke at a few networking meetings and found a few clients there. My social media attracted a few clients too, mainly from LinkedIn.

## Make it a game

Then I played a game called the 90 day money game with some other coaches, where you had to choose an amount of money that you would like to create.

You could not control how much money you made but you could control the amount of conversations you had, so I got to work on offering conversations.

I wondered where I would find these people to have conversations with and came up with lots of ways to reach out to them.

Sometimes I walked around business parks calling into businesses and then talking and listening to the people there. I asked 'what's your biggest challenge?'

Sometimes I would get a business advertising magazine through the door and would ring people up who were advertising in it.

I reached out and offered my conversations on social media and I offered telephone conversations, too. I sat in hotel rooms and talked to strangers about their life. And I reached out directly to people on my friend's lists on the internet.

Reaching out is just the start

I had five people in five days who said they would sign up for coaching, but at the time I had no contracts and they all cancelled. They were not ready and I didn't have the learning back then to consider exploring this a little deeper with them or to test their commitment. What I know now is that when clients are ready you don't really need contracts.

We get it in our heads that we need paperwork, contracts, payment machines, and websites. We don't actually need any of those things.

Overall the most successful of the methods for attracting clients were public speaking, blogging and LinkedIn. Later I found clients through other social media channels.

I coached hundreds of people over the course of that challenge.

Get clarity

Today I do things a little differently. I'm clear now as to who my ideal clients are, so I'm no longer trying to coach everyone or marketing my services towards everyone. I'm very focussed about it. I've reverted back to sending out five letters a week.

The first week I spoke to the director of a global company and we met for a conversation. The second week I sent one letter to the wrong person, as they were on the board of directors but not the owner, I spoke to the person on the phone who already provided coaching for their clients, when I spoke more he asked me to visit for a meeting.

Sometimes things really are simple but we think they can't possibly be and over complicate them.

They invited me to speak at a breakfast meeting and we spoke of possible courses.

# 'I'M NOT LIKE THESE PEOPLE'

I have both said this in the past and heard others say it, but it's how we create separation. We may seem separate on the surface, but we are connected when we go deep. We are all at different points on our journey and slowing down has certainly helped me to find more connectedness with everyone, not just people at similar points of their journey or with similar goals.

What are you basing this on?

If we base it just on appearances then we haven't got to know them.

When we have a conversation we find out all sorts of wonderful things about them. If we are vulnerable and open up to them they do too. We get to listen to their language and find out where they are on their journey. Every person is a door to another world, but not everyone is ready to open the door.

## People will hold me back

The more you believe in yourself and your dream the less you will allow yourself to be held back, but it's hard to move forward in a negative environment.

## I don't want to be around negativity

Sometimes negativity is a great motivator. We have all heard to let your haters be your motivators. Use it. What's hard is the frustration you feel inside when you come across negativity, but sometimes what these people are saying is a lesson you haven't learnt yet.

## I want a positive environment

Positive environments are easier on us, as when others believe in us we can believe in ourselves. Everything is energy, so being in positive environments helps.

Be around more positive influences.

Maybe you are at the stage where you want people around you who you can learn from? I have learnt that my energy and how I feel are two of the most important aspects of my working with others. So, I'm not prepared to compromise my energy by surrounding myself with people I could help, but who aren't ready to help themselves. Love them, bless them and release them; they have their own journey to take first.

Maintaining positive energy is easier when you aren't faced with the frustration of other people's limitations. Frustration hides the opportunity to get curious.

- Anything is possible

- Have a can do attitude and a positive mindset

- Keep growing

- Want more ease

- It's great to want more for yourself. You are worthy of it

## WHO ARE YOU MARKETING YOUR SERVICES TO?

Something that I'm noticing is that often entrepreneurs with high level skills and knowledge spend a lot of time marketing to the masses rather than specifically the clients they want to attract.

This often requires clarity, focus and a mindset shift.

I suspect, also, that as we are often conditioned to be nice we grow up wanting to help everyone.

<u>You cannot help those who aren't ready. Serve them instead and let them find their own way.</u>

I know myself that I have come across points in my journey where the lesson was to leave people behind, which was scary, but that I also realised that when I stepped up or shifted my services towards different clients the people I was moving away from didn't notice or make a fuss anyway.

This inability to step up and leave people behind was within me. Do you feel it too?

What would people think if I suddenly started marketing my services to the minority, started talking more about strategy and about the taboo subject of money?

What I realised was that the very thing I was afraid of stepping up into was what my ideal clients wanted to hear.

I was meant to work at a higher level because I have grown to that level. I need to work where I can be of most use and that isn't helping those who aren't ready yet.

Sometimes we ask ourselves who we can help. What if no one needs helping, but to serve others you step up into your best self and inspire them to do that too.

I mean, who do we really help by playing small? Often the people we are trying to help have to realise they can move themselves first, then they can move more powerfully. This is, in fact, their responsibility. Sure we can encourage, inspire, etc, but we cannot help.

It's not our place to rush people on their journey and to meet them where they are at doesn't help us. I believe you have to find those who are meeting you where you are in terms of readiness and willingness, in terms of action taking and fearlessness.

## Patterns

You see, I'm noticing patterns. The people who became my clients are ready. They are willing, they take responsibility and they also know it's up to them to do the work.

They either understand the process or are willing to trust it. They want to feel good, to be around good energy and leaders. Life is full of people who feel bad, whose energy is negative.

People want to feel good about themselves.

## Pain and pleasure

We are all moving away from pain and moving towards pleasure. We need both. If you are just moving away from pain you don't get anywhere or any growth. So, you need to create the pleasure to pull you forward too. That's where having a dream goal or vision comes in.

If you don't know what that is you are probably just moving away from pain.

## Reactive or proactive?

Do you move because of circumstances or outside influences, or are you constantly making strides to move towards your goals?

My clients are either already moving towards pleasure or have totally had enough of pain and are willing to try something else.

Back to marketing, who are your ideal clients and are you really marketing to them? Specifically?

<u>Are you speaking your client's language?</u>

The secret is that you get to a certain point in the journey and you realise that your ideal client is you.

Are you marketing to you?

Not you before, but you right now at this moment.

What marketing are you attracted to?

What hooks you in?

Something I have noticed is that my ideal clients want what I want, they have similar interests values and aren't afraid to do the work.

These are my 10 out of 10s. They are willing to move beyond comfort and go after what they want; they are willing to do whatever it takes to get there. They are superstars and they get the best results.

Whether this is being open, slowing down, stepping up .... the list goes on. They don't say 'I can't', they say 'ooh I'll do it'. They love growth. They love feeling good. They love achieving.

However, their love of all this can get in their way, too.

# **YOUR JOURNEY TAKES YOU FULL CIRCLE**

When you are awake to all of this you arrive at the start

Until I was in my early twenties I lived in a semi-detached house in a rural area.

It had a rough back lane, full of potholes, where I would ride my Raleigh denim bicycle. It was, and still is, surrounded by fields and mountains where we would explore, make camps, have picnics and adventures.

When I got to my teens living so far off the main road became a problem. My parents wanted me home early and I wanted to explore more exciting places. I had forgotten the excitement of the adventures once experienced there.

Certainty

When I got to my twenties the stability and consistency of 20 years in the same place was too comfortable and safe for me.

I sought out exciting new people and places, and grew to love uncertainty and growth. I wanted the excitement of cities and towns.

Recently I've been learning, through writing, to accept and be happy with where I am right now and it's been amazing.

Often we go through phases in our lives where we are not happy where we are or we are striving for more, but where we are is the one place we belong in each moment. Being present with ourselves and our surroundings in the moment is the key to living life. It's also the key to a successful business.

It's where we find ourselves in each moment of everyday.

We can have dreams and take action to create these but we must not let those dreams take over the happiness that we can feel in the current moment, or when we get there we may have lost more than we have gained.

Long term mindset with presence

We often work hard so that we can go on holidays to escape for short periods and rest, but in being fully present there is no need to escape and in being at peace with ourselves we do not need to rest because we are living. When we are in flow, things are more balanced.

We only need to rest when we are striving and it's hard. Maybe I can say this because I have been on this journey of self-exploration, massive action and building dreams to arrive at this point.

What I know is there is nothing more restful than being and enjoying who and where you are. Being good enough. It shines through your life and through your business.

This week my journey has brought me full circle - to me right here, right now. I have travelled my journey; I have worked hard, created, stepped up and taken a lot of action. This week I am learning to let go and I have met myself face to face.

## Meet yourself where you are

Natasha. Not the coach, not the Womenspirer, not the action taker, but Natasha just as I was before I left the home that I spent 20 years in: happy, fun, easy going and present. Open, loving and living life.

And the amazing thing is that when I leaned into letting go of everything else I was scared, but actually things fall into place and everything works perfectly.

I'm letting go of society's idea of what a business should look like and I'm now redefining what business means to me.

- What does living life mean to you?

- What type of business are you creating?

- Can you have that now?

Because through the course of writing this book I discovered that I can.

I hope that by reading it you can sink into more happiness and ease too, in life and in business. When I started out as a coach I wanted to help everyone, so I was stretched and financially it was a struggle. I didn't know the value of what I provided and because of that I didn't step into that. Not everyone deserves to sit at your table and if you let them you will be stretched too. These days I work with only 15 action taking clients in my one-to-one coaching and the investment for that runs into thousands of pounds.

I now know my worth, and it's life changing. Know your worth, too!

Step up, let go and make sure it's life changing for you, too.

Copyright Natasha Davies 2016

I would love to hear your views and suggested titles, details are below.

I hope you found this book useful.

I would love to hear your comments or suggested book titles, based on any insights you received by reading this book or how you perceived this book.

Please email:

Natashadavies@because-u-can.co.uk

With love and blessings

Natasha

Entrepreneur Mindset Coach and Consultant at Because U Can

*Enjoy your jouney!*

Copyright Natasha Davies 2016

www.ingramcontent.com/pod-product-compliance
Lightning Source LLC
Chambersburg PA
CBHW070235190526
45169CB00001B/187